THE INFLUENCE GAME

50 Insider Tactics
from the Washington, D.C.,
Lobbying World
That Will Get You to Yes

Stephanie Vance

WILEY

John Wiley & Sons, Inc.

Published by John Wiley & Sons, Inc., Hoboken, New Jersey.
Published simultaneously in Canada.

For general information on our other products and services or for technical support, please contact our Customer Care Department within the United States at (800) 762-2974, outside the United States at (317) 572-3993 or fax (317) 572-4002.

Wiley publishes in a variety of print and electronic formats and by print-on-demand. Some material included with standard print versions of this book may not be included in e-books or in print-on-demand. If this book refers to media such as a CD or DVD that is not included in the version you purchased, you may download this material at http://booksupport.wiley.com. For more information about Wiley products, visit www.wiley.com.

Library of Congress Cataloging-in-Publication Data:

Vance, Stephanie, 1966-
      The influence game : 50 insider tactics from the Washington, D.C. lobbying world that will get you to yes / Stephanie Vance.
          p. cm.
      Includes index.
      ISBN: 978-1-118-27159-9 (cloth)
      ISBN: 978-1-118-28359-2 (ebk)
      ISBN: 978-1-118-28497-1 (ebk)
      ISBN: 978-1-118-28727-9 (ebk)
       1. Lobbying—United States.   I. Title.
  JK1118.V36 2012
  324'.40973—dc23

                                                                     2012004736

Printed in the United States of America
10 9 8 7 6 5 4 3 2 1

Contents

Acknowledgments

It's cliche to say that many, many people made this book possible, but it's true so I'll say it anyway. Thousands of citizen advocates, lobbyists, legislators, colleagues, professors, friends, family and general observers of the political scene have taught me everything I know about ethical influence. They've also been incredibly patient with me as I've learned and worked to find the words to express these strategies to others.

I continue to be surprised and encouraged by the number of thoughtful and caring people—yes, even in Washington, D.C.—who have used these tactics to change the world, even where I don't agree with the change they seek to achieve. In fact, I often learn the most from those I agree with the least. It's heartening to know that people from opposite ends of the political spectrum can agree on a principled process for persuasion that works. This gives me hope, not just for governance, but for everyone's ability (including yours!) to influence others honestly and without malice.

Those who observe life know that you won't get very far if you don't know with certainty the lines you won't cross, the principles you hold dear and the steps you are willing to take to achieve your goals. You also won't get far if you sit back, relax and let others do the work. As Robert Kennedy said (far more eloquently than I), "[i]t is not enough to understand, or to see clearly. The future will be shaped in the arena of human activity, by those willing to commit their minds and their bodies to the task." I can honestly say that almost everyone I meet "commits their minds and their bodies to the task." Thank you for showing me how to do so as well.

Don't just be along for the ride. Go forth—and influence.

Introduction

You have to know the rules of the game. And then you have to play it better than anyone else.

—Albert Einstein

Being Heard versus Being Agreed With

In August 2010 citizens stormed congressional town hall meetings, district offices, and even camped out on Capitol Hill, demanding to be heard on the topic of health care. You may recall the whole health care reform debate. The bill being considered was called the "Health Care Affordability and Accessibility for All Act" by those who liked it and "The Job-Killing Health Care Reform Act" or "Obama-Care" by those who didn't.

Regardless of their position, ardent activists put a premium on making their views known. They wrote letters and e-mails, attended town hall meetings, and held large rallies. They shouted through bullhorns, yelled, made threats and, on the positive side, delivered honest heartfelt stories.

Meanwhile, lobbyists from all walks of life (health insurers, medical professionals, patient groups, and the like) walked the halls of Congress seeking to influence the details of the legislation (sometimes in coordination with those storming town hall meetings). For example, tucked into the bill's almost 2,000 pages of new programs and changes to laws was a 12-year exclusivity provision for the biologic drug industry for the manufacture and sale of their drugs. The medical device industry won increased coverage for their products. And lest you think it's all about corporate finagling, one of the biggest winners in the debate was an organization called the Trust for America's Health (TFAH). A relative newcomer, TFAH won significant battles in promoting coverage for services (dubbed "preventive care") designed to limit the onset of chronic diseases, like heart disease and obesity. They achieved this despite their foundation-based funding (not "well-heeled" interests) and, according to lobbying disclosure reports, with just three to four staffers who spent part of their time "lobbying."

These three to four TFAH lobbyists were among the 12,941 registered lobbyists in 2010 roaming the halls of Congress and federal agencies. Beyond health care reform, special interests pushed everything from trade tariffs on coffee beans to shelters for the homeless. Yet in that particular session of Congress only about 4 percent of the 10,809 bills that were introduced actually became law (it should be noted that this statistic does not count the "stand-alone" bills that were passed as attachments to other bills. Nevertheless, the overall percentage of bills passed remains miniscule). What caused some to succeed and others to fail? Some might say bribery and corruption. Some might say logic and reason. But based on my 20-plus years of experience in Washington, D.C., I can tell you that the secret formula used by the victors of 2010 was much more complicated than most people recognize. They incorporated many of the other tactics outlined in this book into their strategy. And I'd be hard-pressed to name a more difficult legislative session in which to win at the influence game.

Whether we're talking about legislators, a corporate board, an employer, a potential customer, a current client, a community advisory committee, or even your spouse, there's a real difference between being heard and being agreed with. Anyone can "be heard." Being agreed with is where the real challenge lies, and no one knows better how to get to that all-important goal than lobbyists and special interests in Washington, D.C.

What This Book Will Tell You

This is not a book about persuading and influencing for its own sake, nor is it about lobbying government. It's about translating the influence strategies we use in Washington, D.C., to get to yes on something you want in the real world, whatever that is—even if it's moving up a rung on the corporate ladder or getting a good deal on a house.

It's also not about whether you agree with the outcome of the policy issues used as examples. Personally, there are some outlined in this book that I don't really like all that much. The purpose is to look at how the lobbyists and special interests associated with the successes won over others, and then to apply those strategies to your own cause.

You're busy, right? In recognition of that fact, this book has been divided into 10 chapters. Within those chapters, a total of 50 "bite-sized" tactics are presented. You will gain benefits from reading one segment or a dozen. Topics include:

- Understanding the principles of influence
- Identifying and articulating your specific goal
- Researching and understanding your audience
- Finding the right people to help make your case
- Gaining access to the right decision makers
- Developing the information and expertise you'll need
- Crafting a winning message
- Utilizing tenacity and persistence to persuade, not annoy

As you review these tactics, you may think they sound familiar—and if you're at all knowledgeable about sales and marketing strategies, you'd be right. In the corporate arena, people sell goods and services. In Washington, D.C., lobbyists sell ideas. It's all sales, but the difference is that the benefits and downsides of ideas are much more difficult to predict and explain. It's generally easy to describe what a widget does—press button A and outcome B is supposed to happen. Depending on how often that outcome really does occur, and assuming that outcome is valuable to the consumer, someone may decide to buy that particular widget.

The selling of ideas, on the other hand, requires a far more subtle and psychological approach. It's not always possible to predict the likely outcome of things like "tax incentives" or "economic development programs." If you start a program to "recruit and maintain effective teachers and principals" (as is one of the goals of a federal grant program called "Race to the Top"), you can't always be sure you'll get the outcome you're looking for. Who is effective? Where are we recruiting them to? Why is this important?

Lobbyists in this example must sell the idea of the "race to the top" as a solution to solve the problem of achievement gaps and to better prepare students for postsecondary and workforce endeavors. The sell isn't just "we need better teachers in underachieving schools," it's "we need to better prepare students for the workforce." In the real world, the kid using a Microsoft product to lobby for a dog wasn't selling dog ownership (see Chapter 2 for details). He was selling protection, responsibility, and good health.

At the same time special interests must convince others that their proposal offers the best solution to a perceived problem. Lobbyists do this every day. They employ their expertise, not only in their topic area, but in the principles of influence, to get what they want, for themselves or their clients. This book shares these secrets with you so that you can use these same strategies to get to "yes."

Influence in the Real World

Starting in second or third grade, and for an extended time after that, I wanted to be a poet when I grew up. Yes, that's true, just ask my parents. By the age of 10, I knew most of T. S. Eliot's work (totally inappropriate for a 10-year-old, by the way) and could recite, almost accurately, parts of *The Odyssey*.

Not surprisingly I did not have many friends as a young child, except for our school librarian, who lit up when I walked through the doors. Invariably, from behind her desk she pulled some book of poetry or mythology designed for young people that none of the other kids (or most of the teachers) would want to read. I could see, even then, that it thrilled her to have a young person so interested in these usually overlooked subjects.

Fast forward 30 to 35 years later when my favorite school librarian would have been unable to hand me that book, not because it was banned, but because it could have the toxic substance lead in it—and apparently there was some danger I might lick it.

How could that happen? In November 2009, school and public librarians across the country were shocked when the Consumer Products Safety Commission (CPSC) proposed requiring all new and existing children's toys, including books, be tested for lead before allowing children to use them.

Clearly, no one wants lead in children's toys. At the same time, however, no one considered the implications for these proposals on libraries. Imagine having to remove every single children's book from the shelves of public and school libraries around the country.

The "rulemaking" process under which the proposals were issued allows for review and comment by the public at large and, of course, lobbyists. That's when the American Library Association (ALA) went to work. They teamed with the Association of American Publishers (AAP)—even though publishers and librarians were at that same time in a "fight to the death," as Emily Sheketoff, executive director of the ALA Washington office put it, over copyright issues.

Attempts to directly engage CPSC leaders through in-person meetings with the ALA's registered lobbyists failed, so the organization turned to its most powerful weapon: its members. Sheketoff approved an action alert asking all library supporters to call the commissioners with a single message—"don't do this." She urged them to tell their stories as well, particularly how the proposal would affect the users of their library. In addition, the ALA suggested library supporters ask their members of Congress to reinforce the message through somewhat strongly worded communications to the agency.

After two days of calls that flooded the phone lines, CPSC staff contacted the ALA and begged them to "call off the dogs." Clearly, the strategy gained their attention and eventually their support. The proposal was fixed four months later after more than a year of delay.

To succeed, the ALA used a variety of influence techniques. In working with the publishers, librarians embraced the idea of "unusual allies" even though the two organizations disagreed vehemently—and at the same time—on another issue. They tried several different strategies, such as direct lobbying and public relations, before alighting on the grassroots tactic that worked. They circled the wagons around a single message. They used all their resources, including those of the organization's "Office for Library Advocacy," which works to support the efforts of advocates seeking to improve libraries of all types. They fought the battle on all fronts.

Most important, they were persistent. They kept going until they achieved their goal—and even after that. When the CPSC told the ALA they would be delaying implementation until the issue was resolved, the librarians used the "trust but verify" tactic to keep the pressure on—gently—until all the *t*'s were crossed and *i*'s dotted.

How does a group of librarians—those people we usually associate with "shushing" in the library—beat back a potentially harmful regulation? They didn't use bribery, manipulation, or lying. They didn't have secret access to smoke-filled backrooms. They didn't even have a huge amount of money behind their campaign. They succeeded because they knew how to play the influence game, and win. How can you use these strategies to your advantage? This book will show you; let's get started.

Chapter 1

Principles of Influence

Rules are not necessarily sacred, principles are.

—**Franklin Delano Roosevelt**

I'm sure the thought of using the words *principles* and *politicians* in the same sentence—especially when we're talking about influence strategies from Washington, D.C.—seems a little odd. We hear of some new scandal every day. In fact, in polls of the most trustworthy professions in America, lobbyists and politicians inevitably rank last.

Yet the most effective lobbyists in Washington, D.C., sleep at night. You may not understand how, especially those who work on issues with which you disagree, but they do. Sure, there are those who cheat their clients, give advice that they know is bad, or even break the law by trying (whether successfully or not) to buy members of Congress. Over the long term, however, these lobbyists simply do not accomplish as much as those who abide by the positive principles of influence outlined in this book.

If you think about it, when and if the unprincipled lobbyists wind up in jail they aren't really being all that effective.

Let's look at the example of a notorious lobbyist you may have heard of—Jack Abramoff. He's the one who went to prison for three and a half years for corruption of public officials, among other things. Before we get into this example, because I'm an ethical person I must disclose that I once worked at a law firm where, several years after I left, Abramoff would become a partner. The firm, then called Preston Gates & Ellis, was implicated in some of his egregious activities. That said, my only direct interaction with him was in a room in the company of about 100 other people. Despite the fact that he and I had no personal connection other than this brief encounter, when the details of the scandal were coming out my parents called frequently to ask, "Have you been subpoenaed yet?"—to which my answer was, "Do you know what *subpoenaed* means? 'Cause it's not good."

I was never subpoenaed, but I did learn at least one important thing in reviewing what happened: in the long run, Jack Abramoff was not a good lobbyist, in any sense of the word. Sure, initially he had some success extracting large sums from various interests (such as online casinos and Native American tribes) in exchange for "influencing" Congress to pass (or not pass) bills favorable to those clients. He lied, he cheated, he bought access, and he bribed.

But did he achieve anything? Perhaps here and there he won some small victories, but a review of some of his policy efforts shows that a version of the online gambling legislation his clients sought to defeat in 1999 was passed in 2006, language to support the Tigua tribe that he bribed Congressman Bob Ney to insert into legislation never passed, he failed to persuade Congress to reopen several Native American casinos, and eventually his efforts to keep the Northern Mariana Islands from being subjected to federal minimum wage laws failed. Oh, and he, his partner, and several other people associated with the scandal went to prison. And did I mention the $1.7 million he owes to the Internal Revenue Service?

In his autobiography *Capitol Punishment,* Abramoff claims that he saved his clients millions of dollars by preventing the passage of certain harmful new taxes and restrictive policies. It's hard to say, though, whether these things would have passed anyway, particularly because Republicans—a party not likely to support many of the taxes and other policy issues Abramoff lobbied against—were in control of both the House of Representatives *and* the Senate almost the entire time, with the exception of the 2001-2002 term, when Democrats barely held on to an evenly divided Senate.

I'm not defending what Abramoff did. His tactics were, indeed, horrible, unethical, and illegal. However, while we tend to believe he had amazing power because he could get in to see those politicians who took his campaign money (he made more than $4.4 million in contributions), in the end things didn't turn out so well for that great influencer Jack Abramoff or, obviously, his clients. As Judy Schneider, a specialist on Congress in the government division of the Congressional Research Service (CRS) and a person who trains members of Congress on the legislative process, says, "That's what people don't get about Abramoff. In the end, he never really accomplished anything."

Contrast Abramoff's story with that of Wayne Pacelle, current president and CEO of the Humane Society of the United States (HSUS) and former vice president for government affairs who, along with his team at HSUS, has overseen the passage of more than 15 federal animal protection statutes and hundreds of state statutes.

Funded by membership dues and contributions, the HSUS, like Abramoff, has a wide range of influence tools at its disposal. Humane USA, an unaffiliated political action committee for the animal protection movement, contributed about $212,000 to political campaigns in the 2010 cycle. HSUS has a cadre of government relations professionals walking the halls of Congress. Their powerful professional grassroots campaign staff helps stoke and fuel communications from citizens to their representatives in Congress. They use earned media, paid advertising, and any legal and ethical tool they can get their hands on to further their cause. I'd bet Wayne Pacelle or his lobbying staff could get in to most offices on Capitol Hill.

Using similar tools, at a much more limited magnitude than Abramoff, the HSUS has achieved some major legislative victories in recent years and, in a very tough budget climate, managed to get record-level increases for animal welfare–related federal programs. How did they succeed? Through a combination of legislative strategy, relationship building and, yes, in some cases, having affiliated groups that support animal-friendly legislators through campaign contributions. Yet Wayne Pacelle is the respected leader of a national organization and Jack Abramoff is a convicted felon.

The differences between Jack Abramoff and Wayne Pacelle can be explained through a basic understanding of what effective influence is—and is not—about.

What Influence Is *Not* About

Many of us see the word *influence* as a dirty word. For example, we don't call guidance counselors "influence" counselors, right? Obviously, the word *guidance* has a much better connotation than the word *influence,* and yet they are synonyms. To influence simply means to effect the actions or opinions of others. The decision as to the value of the effect, with the exception of clearly illegal or immoral activities, is mainly in the eye of the beholder. In other words, the act of influencing itself isn't good or bad: we perceive it as good or bad depending on whether we like the outcome or not.

Clearly the tactics used to influence matter as well. Changing the behavior of others through bribery, for example, is bad. But bribery isn't influence. It's bribery. In fact, there are a host of things that effective lobbyists know have no place in the influence world.

The connection between "influence" and "what those people in Washington, D.C., do" certainly doesn't help. It seems like not a day goes by without hearing of some sort of corruption scandal in which unscrupulous politicians do unscrupulous things to unsuspecting citizens. Yet engaging in these corrupt practices, although they may bring some short-term gain, will not achieve lasting influence. To achieve beneficial long-term benefits, you must know what effective influence is *not* about.

Manipulation

You might have heard someone say, "That person is a good influence on so-and-so," but you've probably never heard, "That person manipulated the other person for the better." Influence is about convincing someone else to do something for a mutual interest. Manipulators, on the other hand, convince someone else to do something solely for their own benefit. Effective lobbyists find that policy "sweet spot" where both the decision makers and the lobbyists feel as if they've won—or, at least, both sides are equally miserable with the outcome. They achieve a win-win or an equal and tolerable lose-lose situation. Although they don't always succeed, you'll find many examples of these throughout the book.

I know it will be a stretch to convince you that the road to a successful political career in Washington, D.C., is paved with good intentions. Sure, lobbyists manipulate policymakers and vice versa every day. Usually they achieve this goal by pretending that a mutual interest exists, even when it doesn't. Over the long term, however, these politicians gain a reputation for double dealing and are universally rejected.

In applying this idea to your own influence situation, consider the differences between manipulation and a win-win scenario. Have you figured out how what you want will truly and honestly benefit everyone involved? And more important, have you figured out whether your solution is really the best fit for your audience? In the long run, if there is not mutual benefit to the proposal, the person you've manipulated over to your viewpoint will realize that, change his or her mind and, possibly, bad mouth you to others.

Bribery

In 2012 a chief of staff I know told me about the time he received an e-mail from a businessperson in the district, regarding a policy issue. The congressman, a strong proponent of business and economic interests, was inclined to support his constituent—except for one sentence in the message: "I've sent in my contribution to the congressman's campaign and look forward to seeing you at the upcoming event."

Because the constituent inadvertently tied support for a policy issue to a campaign contribution, that one sentence ruined his prospects. My friend politely, apologetically, but firmly had to tell the constituent "That's it. We can't help you now. It's not only unethical but illegal." This representative and his staff are on the opposite end of the political spectrum from me (we still play nicely together, though). This strong feeling against even the perception of bribery is bipartisan and ubiquitous.

I realize that many people see bribery as the most pervasive and effective technique for convincing politicians to do something (or not do something, as the case may be). Last time I checked, though, bribery is illegal and most people in Washington, D.C., don't want to take the risk of several years in prison, even a prison for white-collar criminals. As the penalties for a bribery conviction become even more stringent (in 2007, for example, Congressman William Jefferson from Louisiana received a 13-year sentence), politicians become even more nervous.

If you prefer to look at it cynically, think about this: you rarely know if bribery is going to work—and when you attempt it and it doesn't work, you've made an enemy for life and possibly earned yourself a jail term.

In fact, in the wake of all these lobbying scandals, the U.S. Congress passed a series of new rules and regulations designed to dramatically reduce lobbyists' ability to "bribe" elected officials with cash, gifts, or other benefits such as travel. The bill, called the Honest Leadership and Open Government Act, requires lobbyists to fill out a variety of disclosure forms, contribution reporting forms, and the like. The Obama administration got on the bandwagon as well, banning anyone registered as a lobbyist from talking to any executive branch employee. Not only does this make it extremely difficult to share information about the potential impact of new rules and regulations, but dinner table conversation in homes where a lobbyist is married to an executive branch employee has been dramatically impacted.

I'm not suggesting people feel bad for lobbyists because they have to fill out paperwork; however, while imposing important restraints on how the business of Washington gets conducted, these rules do have some unintended consequences. For example, the prohibition on taking a legislator out to dinner has resulted in the toothpick rule, which suggests that any food offered at a lobbyist-sponsored reception in Washington, D.C., must fit on a toothpick. In addition, to eliminate any perception that the reception might equal a meal, lobbyists and policymakers must stand throughout the entire event. Toothpick manufacturers love this rule—chair manufacturers do not.

Regardless of how you feel about toothpicks and chairs, the point is that by both regulation and effective influence practice, bribery simply doesn't work over the long run in Washington, D.C. Money for money's sake is not generally a motivation for policymakers. Members of Congress do seek funds for their reelection campaign but recognize that whereas you need money to run a campaign, you need votes to win an election. And legislators know that voters will not support those convicted of or even tainted by a bribery scandal. It's no coincidence that every lawmaker convicted of bribery—and most accused of it—either lost their seat or resigned shortly thereafter.

Applying the no bribery rule to your cause is usually pretty easy. Just ask yourself, "Am I breaking the law by offering money, gifts, or other benefits solely in exchange for a favor?" If the answer is yes, that's bribery.

Selling Out

I define *selling out* as agreeing to do something (such as taking on a certain job or client) exclusively for the money. While working on Capitol Hill I'd get an interesting phone call at least once per week that went something like this: "Hello, this is the lobbying firm of so-and-so, so-and-so, so-and-so, and so-and-so. We need someone with your expertise and connections on our staff, and we'd like to pay you (insert ridiculous amount of money here)." My husband sometimes wanted me to take these jobs, but I never did because I did not feel strongly about their cause, or in some cases I didn't even support it.

In fact, in 1994, when my then boss was downsized by the voters (a euphemism for the fact that he lost his reelection), I lost my job. After about six weeks of looking I was offered two jobs on the same day. One was for a cause I believed in. One was for a cause I felt indifferent about. The cause I felt indifferent about offered me 50 percent more in salary, but I turned it down. And I'm not the only one who made choices like this. Frankly, I never met one staff person who left Capitol Hill to work for a cause he or she did not feel strongly about or at least support. I certainly didn't agree with many of these causes, but the important thing is that they did. They didn't sell out. Of course, I didn't meet every staff person on Capitol Hill, but in my experience "selling out" is the exception, not the rule.

Logic

Many people believe that if they simply tell a decision maker about their cause and proposed solution, the decision maker will see the light and automatically agree. I see this perspective a great deal with those lobbying on more technical issues, like engineers or scientists. In their world, logic reigns. Once you find the answer to a problem, you apply that answer and the problem is generally solved. If it's not, you need to look for another solution.

Unfortunately, purely logical arguments rarely work in an influence situation because these situations are subjective. The so-called right answer is almost always open to interpretation because different people see the world in different ways. Members of Congress, for example, are more likely to accept logical arguments that benefit their constituents, even if that solution is not in the best interests of the entire country. This is how representative democracy works.

Sure, you'll want to be sure your argument for your cause makes sense. But it will need to make sense from the perspective of your audience, not necessarily in terms of your perspective, or even from the perspective of how it may benefit the world at large. You'll need to put words around your purely logical statement to convince a decision maker that your approach makes sense for *both* logical and self-interested reasons. Chapter 8 will show you how.

Lying

The first time a lobbyist lies to a member of Congress or his staff person is the last. Well, I'll amend that. The first time a lobbyist is *discovered* lying to a member of Congress or a staff person is the last. But those discoveries are made sooner rather than later because information flows so freely in Washington, D.C., sometimes even by accident.

I had this happen to me several times while working on Capitol Hill. People would meet with the congressman and he would say, pretty unequivocally, that such-and-such was not his position on an issue. One group we met with went back to the district and told an outright lie to their members about what the congressman had said. One of their members was a close friend of the congressman and asked him what he had said. Once we discovered the deception, we never met with that group again.

What Influence *Is* About

Overall you'll probably notice that these ideas about what influence is *not* about will differ from the current thinking about a corrupt political system. Even very respected observers of the political process may comment that legislators and their staff are "bought and sold." I can tell you only about what my own experiences in Washington, D.C., are like. My overall goal is not to make you feel better about politics. My goal is to show you what I've seen that works, and doesn't work, on Capitol Hill. And I've seen campaigns based on the following principles work time and time again.

Passion and Conviction

To be successful, you must care, and care deeply, about what you want. Every lobbyist knows that any attempt to influence others on an issue of little importance to him or her will fall flat. The sense of "conviction" you bring to the table dramatically impacts the outcome.

Think about it in the context of sales: if you don't personally believe in the product, you are not likely to get others to do so as well. In Washington, D.C., lobbyists "sell" ideas, and there are as many different ways to care about a policy idea as there are registered lobbyists. Sometimes it's a personally held belief, sometimes it's a desire to promote a specific type of business, or sometimes it's even love for a particular region of the country. As Marci Merola from ALA's Office of Library Advocacy puts it, "People have x-ray vision when it comes to other people's motives." If your motive doesn't have the force of conviction behind it, frankly no one is going to believe you and get on board. Merola calls it the "special spark," and it's critical to success.

To understand this from a D.C. perspective, it's important to understand that there are at least three distinct kinds of lobbyists: lobbyists for hire, lobbyists with a love for their topic, and lobbyists who are lucky enough to earn money for working on a topic they love.

In general, what I describe as lobbyists "for-hire," are those who work for a law or lobbying firm under contract to a specific client. For-love lobbyists are those who are so enthusiastic about an issue that they would advocate on it for free—and in fact some of them do just that. I put so-called citizen lobbyists in this category, specifically those who, although they aren't professionals, become very involved in a particular issue for their own often very personal reasons.

The lobbyists working for both love and money tend to be connected to associations or so-called special interest groups. (By the way, please don't shudder at the term *special interest*. In the next section, we'll talk more about why they really aren't so terrible.)

In my own career, I have been all three kinds of lobbyist. I started shortly after college at a law firm that represented the interests of a range of different clients. For example, I worked closely with one of the lead attorneys for a company called Tele-Communications Inc., or TCI, a cable company that was very involved in efforts to reauthorize the Telecommunications Act. I also worked on a rather random array of issues such as nuclear energy and reinsurance concerns, which are led by the companies that insure insurance companies. Yes, there is a special interest group for everything. The firm was made up of for-hire lobbyists.

In looking at for-hire lobbyists, you may think, "Yeah, they're just passionate about making money"—and some of them are. I'm certainly not suggesting that sweet and pure motives govern every lobbyist, or even that some of those with less-than-altruistic motivations have not been successful. However, the vast majority of successful influencers often start with a profound understanding of—and enthusiasm for—a particular cause. Or, in the case of more esoteric issues, like reinsurance, they may be engaged simply because they love the legislative process. Development of campaign strategies, identification of allies, and the "thrill of the hunt" are the things that get them out of bed in the morning, not necessarily the money.

Later, I worked as a lobbyist for National Public Radio, where all I worked on, day in and day out, was protecting public radio's interests on Capitol Hill, particularly during the debates in early 1995 about eliminating funding for public broadcasting. I love public broadcasting. That's why I took the job, which, believe me, paid a lot less than other positions I was offered.

You also see this for-love enthusiasm with lobbyists associated with disease-focused special interest groups, such as the American Heart Association or the Lupus Foundation of America. The people working for these organizations are passionate about curing diseases. They may currently suffer from or may have recovered from that disease—or they know someone who has.

Sometimes you'll find for-love lobbyists who've been fighting a particular policy battle all their lives, like Lynne Bradley of the American Library Association (ALA). After working as a librarian for many years, she developed a profound level of enthusiasm for life-long learning and the First Amendment. She now serves as director of the ALA's Washington office.

Even those lobbyists associated with trade associations (those made up of individuals representing different kinds of businesses) generally believe that the types of businesses they represent do some good in the world. In some cases their passion may be making the marketplace better for that business. In others, they may believe strongly that removing taxes and regulations on businesses is good for the whole country.

Finally, some lobbyists (like me) are lucky enough to work for both love and money. Since 2000 my focus has shifted to what is known as grassroots lobbying, although I do represent a couple of clients on Capitol Hill—just to keep up with the latest twists and turns in the D.C. insider game. Although we are for hire, our firm never takes on a lobbying client whose views we don't feel good about.

As you apply this principle to your own situation, ask yourself why you are willing to spend your valuable time on your cause. Is it love? Money? A combination of both? The answer to these questions will reveal to you your passion. Without your own lasting and authentic conviction that what you want matters, you'll never convince others it's a good idea. It's also unlikely that you'll outlast the many perils of your journey to success. Understanding your own motivation behind your influence effort will help you stay in the game for as long as it takes to succeed.

Reason

As Ben Franklin said, "If passion guides you, let reason hold the reins." In identifying your passion please don't go overboard. There's passion and then there's obsession. Every good lobbyist knows the location of that invisible line, and never crosses it. Those that do are rarely successful.

Nothing demonstrates this better than a meeting I had with a lobbyist from an environmental group bent on protecting old-growth forests in the Pacific Northwest. At the time, I was working for a very "green" member of Congress (i.e., recognized as a supporter of the environment). He had supported this group's position on every vote and every bill. He was very much "for" trees.

But the lobbyist didn't think my boss was doing enough for this group's position. He wanted more action on our part, including making public statements, introducing bills, and demanding certain funding levels. He begged, he pleaded, he wheedled, and he cajoled. He wept over the fate of the trees. Finally, he became so impassioned that by the end of one of our meetings he was pounding on the table, berating our staff, and insisting that he would bring the wrath of the environmental community down on our heads if we didn't comply. The congressman politely but firmly told him to leave and never darken our door again.

Needless to say, this lobbyist did not get what he wanted. However, had he been reasonable by, for example, asking us to take one additional step instead of seventeen, over time he likely would have seen a dramatic increase in our activity on the issue.

One of those for-love citizen lobbyists who lived in our congressional district understood this principle well. Her cause was animal welfare and at the time, she never received a dime for her work. I'm sure her involvement even cost her money.

This advocate (let's call her Kelly, as that was her name) called me before every congressional vote on animal welfare issues. Whether it was allowing military handlers to adopt their war dog partners or boycotting Canada for not preventing the slaughter of Canadian seals, she was on the phone with me two or three days before the vote telling me her opinion and asking for the congressman's support one way or the other.

The entire staff loved animals, so the congressman, to avoid a mutiny, consistently voted the animal welfare party line. However, a vote to ban the practice of whaling by Native American tribes caused some real problems. *Whaling,* for those unfamiliar with it, is the Native American tradition of hunting whales and using those resources for sustenance throughout the year.

The tough part for us was that the congressman's district included a number of tribal areas. Although they were not technically constituents, because tribes are considered separate nations, we were loath to interfere with their culture and the congressman wound up voting against the measure.

Kelly expressed her disappointment, reiterated her reasons for supporting the bill, let us know that she would be sharing our position with others in the district, and said she hoped we'd be able to agree on other issues in the future. That was it. No fist-pounding or yelling. She was passionate about the issue, but let reason guide her actions. After that, we voted with her perspective 100 percent of the time, and eventually the congressman even changed his mind on the issue that started it all. In fact, I later heard she was so good at the influence game that she was hired by the Humane Society of the United States (HSUS) to train other citizen advocates.

As you apply this principle to your own effort, ask yourself how you can reduce concerns that you might be a little *too* passionate about your cause. What factual evidence can you use to back up your argument? Why would someone else want what you want? Balance your passion with your reason. Passion will keep up your spirits through a long and arduous process. It will lend a credibility and authenticity to your voice. Reason will serve to put your passion into the realm of reality so you can avoid ongoing disappointment.

Ethics and Honesty

At the time of my marriage in 1996, I was working for a member of the U.S. House of Representatives. To ensure my compliance with ethics rules, I requested (and received) a letter from the Office of Congressional Ethics approving my receipt of wedding gifts. Even though absolutely no one at my wedding was a registered lobbyist, I asked for this letter to avoid any appearance of impropriety (and, incidentally, I framed this letter and left it on the gift table so everyone would feel perfectly comfortable in their gift-giving). Sure, wedding gifts are discussed in some detail on page 82 of the U.S. House of Representatives' Code of Ethics manual, which is 456 pages long. But one can never be too careful, especially when it comes to the gift rules.

Believe it or not, most policymakers and their staff go to great lengths to protect themselves from any suggestion of an ethical breach.

17

Lobbyists do the same. Although violations of the code of ethics certainly occur, the consequences of such violations are so dire that the vast majority of people in D.C. do all they can to keep their reputations intact.

In addition, valuable political relationships must stand the test of time, and time translates to trust. Every lobbyist knows that if a member of Congress violates the ethics rules he or she runs the risk of reprimand or even expulsion, depending on the level of misconduct. The House Ethics Committee conducted more than 70 investigative hearings from 2009 to 2010 and filed more than 15,000 pages of reports on matters before its jurisdiction. Frankly, no one wants to be mentioned anywhere in those 15,000 pages, which is why effective lobbyists recognize and respect Congressional Ethics rules—and will never ask members of Congress to violate them.

As you're applying the ethics principle to your own cause, ask yourself whether what you want (or perhaps more important, how you're getting it) violates any ethical boundaries. Do you feel good about what you're doing? Are you being honest with others? Is someone agreeing with you and taking action simply because you're paying him or her? Can you tell your mother what you're doing? The answers to any of these questions will tell you whether you've crossed a line.

Relationships

Winners of the influence game thrive on one-on-one relationships, whether professional, personal, or somewhere in between. Many professional lobbyists work on Capitol Hill early in their careers and then parlay that experience into ongoing relationships with staff and/or legislators. Some get to know newer staff and members by helping them understand a particular policy issue or region better. Others have personal connections through friends or family members. And, yes, some build these relationships by attending fundraisers in the hope that the person running for election will remember them when he or she gets into office.

People in Washington, D.C., work hard to build these relationships because they know they will dramatically increase the potential for success. Note that I refer to these as "built" relationships: in other words, they do not simply emerge out of thin air. Tactic 21 ("Don't Network—Netplay," see Chapter 6) discusses the idea of relationship building in more detail. For now, just know that built relationships are essential to any successful influence effort.

Individuals

According to a study by the Congressional Management Foundation, personal visits from constituents influence members of Congress more than any other factor. That's right: more than visits from lobbyists (number five on the list), more than hordes of postcards and e-mails, and more, even, than campaign contributions. In fact, 97 percent of the offices surveyed indicated that constituent visits have a great deal or some influence on key policy decisions, such as how to vote or what bills to support.

The story of Erin Brockovich, as told in the movie of the same name, shows the power of the individual in fighting for a cause. This brash, single mother started (and won) a campaign against a large California power company accused of polluting the groundwater. Her efforts resulted in the federal Superfund law, which focuses on cleaning up hazardous waste sites.

If you doubt whether a single individual can still make a difference in today's corrupt political world, consider the example given by Bradford Fitch, president and chief executive officer of the Congressional Management Foundation. He tells the story of a citizen who showed up for as many of a senator's town hall meetings as he could get to with one message: Medicare was paying too much for a medical device he used. He'd shopped around and found a better price. Eventually, the senator championed the cause, and legislation was eventually adopted changing the standards and reducing the costs. It would be naïve to say that the medical device industry wasn't involved. It would be inaccurate to say the constituent who politely and persistently approached his senator wasn't instrumental to the success.

Crowds

Whereas individuals can make a difference, the combination of individuals and crowds is an almost unstoppable force. All 140,000-plus special interest groups in the United States have one thing in common: they have a special interest. Yes, that seems obvious, but have you ever really thought about it? Those millions of people associated with those thousands of groups come together in support of specific issues or goals. They have organized themselves around a shared enthusiasm that reflects their passion for the change they want to see in their lives and the lives of others.

Take the example of the Lupus Foundation of America, which combines the best of the powers of the individuals and crowds. The members of its national network of chapters, branches, and support groups across the country have come together in support of improving the quality of life for people with lupus. With both individuals and chapters involved, they can generate not only direct patient stories, but lots of them. This approach has resulted in a wide range of successes, including funding for the establishment of a national public awareness campaign through the U.S Department of Health and Human Services aimed at populations most at risk for lupus.

As you apply these principles to your own influence situation, think about whether and how you can combine the power of individuals and numbers. Tactics 19 through 23 in Chapter 6 will help guide the way.

Perseverance

In his iconic work *The Dance of Legislation,* Eric Redman described the inner workings (or nonworkings) of the U.S. Congress. He estimated that it takes an average of seven years to pass a bill through the legislative process. Sure, it's an estimate, and perhaps an inaccurate one at that, but this much is true: it often takes a long time to succeed.

Dave Wenhold, former president of the American League of Lobbyists and partner at Miller/Wenhold Capitol Strategies, a lobbying firm in Washington, D.C., stresses the importance of perseverance when talking about influence. As a lobbyist for the National Court Reporters Association (NCRA), Dave recognized that opportunities existed for his clients in a government mandate that all television programming be closed-captioned by 2006.

Turns out, court reporters are the ones who do the closed-captioning. The mandate highlighted the fact that these highly skilled workers are in short supply. To solve this problem, Dave suggested the NCRA ask Congress to establish a federal program that would increase the pool of court reporters available to undertake this work. Seeing this as a win-win (court reporters win, the hearing impaired win, government wins), Senator Tom Harkin (D-IA) first introduced S. 2512, the Training for Real Time Writers Act, on May 14, 2002.

From 2002 to 2010 the legislation was reintroduced every two years (bills that don't make it through the process in that time frame "die" and must be "reincarnated" in the next session). It garnered more and more support and even passed the Senate twice. Hearings were held, votes were taken, and legislators had nothing but nice things to say. Court reporters from across the nation came to Washington, D.C., every year to lobby in support of the legislation. They met with legislators at home. They begged. They pleaded. But after seven years nothing had become law.

Dave pointed out all along that a political regime change would be necessary to get the bill through the long and arduous process. But after seven years his clients came to him and said, "Can we lobby on something else? We're tired of this issue. It isn't going anywhere." Feeling a responsibility to give them the best advice he could, Dave said, "We shouldn't stop. Let's press on. We're on the cusp." One year later the bill passed. After eight years, the court reporters had won a $100 million grant program.

What would have happened if they had stopped the effort in year seven? Members of Congress would likely have moved on to priorities put forth by others. Through perseverance, the NCRA won the influence game—to the tune of $100 million. Could you use $100 million? I certainly could.

What is true for the legislative process is true for life in general. As the proverb goes, "The darkest hour is just before the dawn." Too many would-be influencers give up right before they are about to succeed. Don't make that mistake.

Relevance

As you've probably discovered, many people make decisions based on self-interest. This does not mean that these decisions are bad or wrong or not altruistic in any way (although some are). It simply means that someone has done a very good job of convincing the decision maker that his or her support for a particular cause is in his or her best interest. And the only way you're going to be able to even begin that process is by establishing your relevance.

In the political arena, this often means explaining why your special interest can help a member of Congress get reelected (or perhaps to explain why your lack of support would be detrimental to reelection). In my days on Capitol Hill I ran into some nontraditional players who are very good at this, such as the American Radio

Relay League (ARRL), which represents the interests of ham radio operators.

You'd never think of this group as a well-heeled special interest, right? In fact, you've probably never thought of this group at all. Those of us who grew up in a noncomputer era may be more familiar with these technology enthusiasts than others. Basically, ham radio operators connect to one another and the world through radio technology. Through a variety of tests designed to demonstrate their extensive knowledge and responsible use of the airwaves, they earn a license to use what are known as the amateur bands of the radio spectrum.

Unfortunately, many people think of amateur radio operators as, frankly, somewhat odd people who sit around in their basements saying "breaker, breaker" into a microphone all day. Nothing could be further from the truth. In fact, amateur radio operators play an essential role in providing emergency communications after natural disasters, such as hurricanes, tornadoes, and earthquakes. After major events such as Hurricane Katrina, or the earthquake and tsunami that devastated most of eastern Japan, ham radio operators were some of the only communication resources available to emergency responders.

You're probably wondering why I know so much about ham radio operators. Well, it turns out that these airwaves—the same ones used by cell phone companies, commercial and public radio, and over-the-air television (remember that?)—are regulated by a federal agency known as the Federal Communications Commission (FCC). And my first boss on Capitol Hill served on a committee that oversaw the activities of the FCC. That's why the government affairs director for the ARRL came to visit me one day regarding a volunteer licensing issue with the FCC. I'll confess, I was not particularly enthusiastic to be meeting with this group. I really didn't know anything about them and was a little frustrated that they were taking up time in my already busy day.

However, my frustration turned to enthusiasm when the first words out of the lobbyist's mouth were, "We have 5,000 members in your district." Our congressional district had one of the highest numbers of ham radio operators of any legislative district in the country. Through that one sentence, that lobbyist immediately demonstrated the relevancy of his organization to the self-interest of both my boss—who wanted to represent his constituents well and, if you're cynical, get reelected—and me, who wanted to keep my job. In addition, the idea of promoting emergency communications seemed very much in the interest of the country at large, not just our constituents.

Clearly this lobbyist knew why he wanted to talk to me: we were in a position to help him with his cause. What made the meeting so memorable was that he immediately made it clear to me why I would want to meet with him. Plus, they put me on the cover of *American Radio Relay League* magazine. It made my year.

Authenticity (or Charm)

Decision makers need to feel positively about you and what you have to offer. Unfortunately, those positive feelings do not automatically result from someone simply knowing about you and your cause. You'll need to wheedle, coax and, yes, charm your way into the person's good opinion.

In Washington, D.C., some people confuse charming with smarmy. Lobbyists have a reputation for a style of fake charm associated with snake oil salesmen. Many believe that lobbyists slink their way into congressional offices with a wink-wink and a nudge-nudge (and, of course, a big campaign check). The truth is that though some lobbyists do try it, this tack usually proves wildly unsuccessful. It's clear that the lobbyist is being nice only because he or she wants something.

What is real charm? I like to consider it in the same way Justice Potter Stewart defined pornography in *Jacobellis v. Ohio:* "I can't describe it, but I know it when I see it." All I know is that real charm comes from a real place. Charming people feel a personal connection to their cause and, to put it simply, are nice. They also look for ways to create win-wins for both sides. People always know when you're being nice just to get what you want. So find that real reason why you want something and be as nice as you can be in asking for it. That's a good start.

Action

Let's say you've reached a point where a decision maker knows who you are and what you do. He or she feels positively about all that. But they're called decision makers for a reason. They make decisions. And they're not going to do that until you ask them to take an action.

As a congressional staff person I had too many people come to our office to "educate" us on an issue. Think back to some of those times when you were educated or, worse, when you were *told* you were being educated—like maybe in your eighth-grade algebra class. What kinds of feelings did that evoke? Resentment? Boredom? I don't know about you, but one of the first things that popped into my head when people said I was going to be educated was, "Will this be on the test?" Frankly, I wasn't planning to write down the information until someone told me I had to do something with it.

Similarly, in an influence situation, the "ask" triggers that little switch in someone's head that says, "Hey, I'm going to have to do something with this information so I better pay attention." That ask equals the sell, and it applies whether you're selling a product, a service, or an idea. Sometimes you'll need to make a series of asks over time to promote an attachment to your cause. In D.C., special interests frequently ask a legislator to make a statement in support of their issue or support a "National 'Whatever' Week" resolution before asking them for something more controversial They reason that the more time and energy the legislator spends on a cause, the more their potential for success increases.

Know the Difference Between a Good Cause and a Special Interest

In Washington, D.C., the difference between a good cause and a special interest is simple: you agree with the policy perspective of a good cause and the other side is always represented by one of those horrible special interests.

Everyone has a special interest and hence everyone *is* a special interest. It's just that your special interest may be diametrically opposed to another's. Or, more likely, others may not be convinced that your interest is in the best interest of everyone else. It's not. That's why it's a special interest. If it were good for everyone it would be a common interest.

To be influential you must give up the idea that your special interest (or your self-interest) is bad or unworthy because it doesn't coincide with everyone else's. Perhaps more important, you must recognize that other people may have good intentions, even when they disagree with you. Your job is to promote your special interest, without vilifying the interests of others, in adherence to the principles of honesty, integrity, and ethics outlined at the beginning of this book.

Chapter 2

Know What You Want

If you don't know where you're going, you'll wind up somewhere else.

—Yogi Berra

L obbyists and regular people differ in many ways, the least of which is that successful lobbyists know with breathtaking clarity what they want. That's because they know that it is very, very difficult to influence someone to give you what you want if you're not sure what that is yourself.

When I was working on Capitol Hill, a college student in our district made the mistake of not knowing what she wanted when she called our office to get every piece of information we had on a controversial foreign aid issue (never mind that she was calling the day before her paper was due). I tried to get her to explain exactly what she needed: Information on legislation introduced? Funding? Agency action? How many letters we'd received on the issue? The politics behind the situation? The various policy issues associated with it? As you can see, there are always many angles to any one issue.

Her response to my questions was, "Just everything you have." So I faxed her 200 pages (this was in the days before e-mail) and I never heard from her again (not even a thank you!). Sure, she got something out of us, but what she received could not have been at all useful to her given her situation. Because she did not know what she wanted (and was trying to figure it out at the last minute), she was not able to adequately frame her request to us.

People want a lot of things. To get the things we want, we often need someone to say yes to something. If you want to start a business, for example, you may need a bank to say yes to a loan, or customers to say yes to a service, or your spouse to say yes to taking on the bills while you get started.

Some wants are more important than others. In fact, some wants rise to the level of needs, often not by accident but as a result of the diligent work of effective special interests. How many times have you heard someone around you say, "I really need this"? Your kids may say they need a cell phone or a dog. Your spouse may say she needs a certain movie package on cable or that he needs a certain piece of kitchen equipment. Your friend may say that she needs a new house. I do this all the time, convincing myself that I really need the latest technological gadget. There's even a current TV commercial from Microsoft starring a precocious child who offers up a slide show to his family explaining why they need a dog. His reasons? Protection for the family, teaching the child responsibility, and extending everyone's life span—good old-fashioned American values. How could they *not* say yes?

In any influence situation, issues perceived as needs tend to get more attention, as in "we need to extend tax breaks for certain business interests in order to spur the economy," or "we need to increase health care coverage for the uninsured." I characterize these as perceived needs not because I disagree with the statements (it doesn't really matter whether I agree or not), but because I want to illustrate the point that this is what lobbying is about—perception. Lobbyists and special interests exist because they want everything from government dollars to starting or closing federal programs to changes in regulations. And their special expertise is in spinning their wants as needs.

Tactic 1: Your Effort Is a Cause

To move from want to need, you must embrace the outcome you seek as a cause. Your cause may be getting a new job, making a sale, or getting a raise. Your cause may even be getting a policymaker to pay attention. Whatever your cause, you are promoting a specific result over opposition, competition, or potential objections.

Consider the causes associated with lobbyists and special interests in Washington, D.C. Some issues, such as helping veterans or homeless people or perhaps passionately defending free speech or free enterprise, are pretty easy to recognize as a "cause." Other concerns, such as a specific tax provision or earmark, may be based on more selfish goals and hence more difficult to see as a "cause." Regardless, whatever motivates people seeking to influence a particular outcome, they will think of their interests as causes. This level of enthusiasm is needed to play and win the influence game. This is why throughout this book I'll refer to any influence situation as a cause—and you should as well.

That said, there's a big difference between trying to pass legislation that would, for example, reform our entire financial industry, and trying to pass legislation that would establish a Civil War Sesquicentennial Commission Act (commemorating that war's 150th anniversary). Big causes will likely take more time, money, effort, and organization, and will likely use many more of the tactics outlined in this book. Smaller, more personal causes, like persuading the family to get a dog, still might not be easy, but they probably won't require a campaign plan that contemplates massive organizing of hundreds or thousands of people.

Once you know both what your cause is and its scope, start playing the influence game by picking a priority and applying the tactics discussed in this book. Pick and choose the tactics that work best for your situation. If you want to convince a bank to loan you several million dollars to start a business, you're probably going to need to develop a more comprehensive long-term effort than if you're trying to get a good deal on a new car.

You'll get started by learning the nature of what you're selling.

Tactic 2: Know the Nature of What You're Selling

With your priority firmly in place, you'll need to figure out the nature of what you're selling. No matter what you're asking for—time, money, resources, patience—it's a sales situation. The nature of your sale varies in intent, scope, importance, and time frame. Your understanding of these factors will impact the depth and breadth of your campaign. Let's look at each of these factors.

Intent: Action or Inertia

Sometimes you'll want the decision maker to do something. Sometimes you'll want the decision maker to *not* do something or, in fact, to do nothing. As you develop your influence campaign, know from the outset whether you're pushing for action or inertia. It won't surprise you to hear that in Washington, D.C., inertia is almost always the easiest to achieve. Special interests often succeed simply by persuading Congress that the status quo is better than any changes legislators could come up with.

This was the approach lobbyists took with efforts to prevent consideration of the Employee Free Choice Act, the so-called card-check legislation. In 2007 the Democratic leaders of both the House and the Senate proposed changing the rules for how unions could organize workers. Supporters, such as unions, argued that the legislation would help workers. Opponents, mainly the business community, argued it would hurt management. The U.S. Chamber of Commerce opposed consideration of the bill, in essence favoring inertia over action. Inertia has won so far, due in part to the change in the political environment in the last couple years.

Inertia in Washington, D.C., has become such a way of life that even the bills that *must* be passed, such as the appropriations bills that keep the government funded, never actually pass on time. And when I say never, I mean never. They have not passed on time even once in the last decade.

Depending on an interest group's perspective, however, promoting action may be more useful, as demonstrated by the Chamber of Commerce's shift in strategy on another issue. When what were known as the Bush Tax Cuts were slated to expire on December 31, 2010, Congress needed to take specific action to extend them. Not surprisingly, legislators disagreed on the best approach. Democrats suggested continuing only those cuts aimed at lower-income individuals. Republicans pushed to maintain the reductions in estate and capital gains taxes, which were generally believed to benefit the well-off.

Both sides agreed on the need for action, but they focused on very different messages to achieve their end goals. After much debate and compromise an extension bill passed on December 15, 2010—just 15 days before the deadline.

In each case, groups like the U.S. Chamber of Commerce developed different messages and took different actions to promote either action or inertia depending on the outcome they sought. You'll need to do the same.

Scope: Controversial or Easy

The ideas lobbyists sell range from large to small, from controversial to uncontroversial, from easy to tough, and everywhere in between. For example, passing legislation designating the U.S. Postal Service facility in Little Ferry, New Jersey, as the Sergeant Matthew J. Fenton Post Office (passed and sent to the president on December 23, 2011) requires less time and political capital than passing legislation changing the tax code or the structure of the financial system.

Controversial decisions tend to generate more opposition as well, and even those items that might not seem all that controversial can turn out that way. Think of your influence effort as existing along a spectrum from easy to difficult, particularly in terms of your audience's perspective. Will it cost them money? Time? Political or other capital? Will someone be angry with them if they agree with you? The answer to these questions will tell you whether the influence situation is controversial or relatively easy.

Importance: Must-Do versus May-Do Decisions

With the right strategy, must-do-soon decisions can be some of the easiest to influence. Take the example of government responses to natural disasters. These situations tend to generate a fair amount of lobbying activity outside the scope of the natural disaster because special interests know that *this* legislation will move quickly, unlike 96 percent of the bills introduced in a year.

In 2006, for example, when the U.S. Congress passed emergency legislation to help provide additional assistance to victims of Hurricane Katrina, the bill included billions of dollars for other totally unrelated programs, such as farm bailouts and research into the threats from bird flu. Lobbyists and special interests saw these bills as opportunities to move their priorities because they were must-do decisions. No legislators wanted to be against relief to victims of Hurricane Katrina, so they agreed to overlook the tacked-on items. Likewise in 2012, legislation to extend a payroll tax benefit included provisions to "study the use of state and local 9-1-1 service charges," as well as funds to conduct research into wireless public-safety communications (all part of a bill called the "Next Generation 9-1-1 Advancement Act" that had been introduced separately earlier in the session). Employment taxes and 9-1-1 services may not seem connected, but in this case they were because government sales of wireless spectrum were being used to offset the cost of the tax break – and because some shrewd politicians took advantage of an opportunity resulting from a "must do" decision.

For your own influence situation, consider whether the decision is a must do or a may do. Does the decision maker desperately need what you're selling right away? Or is it the kind of situation where your product, service, or time would be nice to buy but it's not an absolute essential?

Time Frame: Short-Term or Long-Term

The fast turnaround time also made it easier for special interests to attempt to piggyback their pet projects onto the Katrina legislation. Some decisions are made within a few days. In those cases, it's much easier to get decision makers to just go with the flow because they simply do not have time to consider an alternative option.

Time frame impacts both the types of strategies you use as well as how extensively you use them. A couple hours of research might be appropriate for a decision to be made within a few weeks, whereas several weeks (and, indeed, ongoing analysis) would be appropriate for causes that will take several years to finalize one way or another. At the same time, you may need to build a foundation over time in order to take advantage of a "spur of the moment" opportunity. U.S. Representative Shimkus (R-IL) introduced the "9-1-1 Improvement Act" in July of 2011. He and his allies were well positioned—and early on.

Overall, when playing the influence game, recognize that getting a yes is easier in some situations than others, depending on the various factors noted above. The easiest approvals to win tend to be short-term must-do decisions that are noncontroversial and not action-oriented. On the more difficult end of the spectrum are

Know What You Want

controversial, optional decisions that require your decision maker to take proactive action.

Knowing these four key factors about the yes you're seeking will help you figure out the appropriate strategy. For example: Being hired for a job you've applied for is probably (1) relatively short term (a few months, perhaps), (2) not incredibly controversial (although there may be opposition), (3) a near must-do for the decision maker (or why would they be hiring?), and (4) action-oriented.

If the achievement of your yes is on the more difficult side of the spectrum, you may want to consider building a strategy based on gaining a series of small yeses to lead up to a big one. Lobbyists employ this tactic frequently. They ask legislators to do several relatively easy things related to a controversial issue—for example, to make a statement or schedule time for a meeting—that, over time, increase the policymaker's investment in the outcome and hence his or her likeliness to agree.

Specific Takeaways

If you take away any lessons from this tactic they should be:

- Figure out what you want—even if it's not yet fully articulated. (Chapter 8 will help put words around the ask.)

- Before you develop your strategy be prepared to answer the following questions:

  - Is this an action ask or an inertia ask?

  - Is this ask controversial or easy?

  - Is your ask related to a must-do decision? Or can it be attached to a must-do decision?

  - When does the decision need to be made? If it's long term, are there smaller asks you can make along the way to encourage engagement and commitment?

Tactic 3: Set a SMART Goal

To take the concept of figuring out what you want to the next level, you must have a goal, and not just any goal—a SMART goal. This step (articulated by George Doran, Arthur Miller, and James Cunningham in an article in the November 1981 issue of *Management Review*) increases the specificity of your ask and ensures that you have a good sense of whether you're achieving what you set out to do.

As you've probably surmised, SMART is an acronym. We are very into acronyms in Washington, D.C., which may be why SMART caught on like wildfire with politicians. Or it may have something to do with the fact that it's an excellent place to start with your persuasion strategy.

Depending on who you talk to, the letters may stand for different words, but the meanings are generally the same. SMART goals are specific, measurable, attainable/achievable, relevant/realistic, and timely. If your goal does not have these characteristics, you may find yourself wandering all over the map, without a good sense of which people you should approach, how you should approach them, and what you'll do once you reach them.

Let's look at each of the elements of a SMART goal, and see what we can do to help you build this kind of goal.

Specific

A specific goal answers the what, when, and where questions, such as:

- What do we want?
- When do we want it?
- Where does it need to happen and/or who needs to make the decision?

The answers to these questions help special interests like the National Stroke Association, with a mission to reduce the incidence and impact of stroke, to create effective campaign strategies for their cause. To answer the question of what they want, they developed both a broad and a narrow policy agenda. The broad agenda laid out some overall concept goals, such as increasing the percentage of federal funds allocated to stroke research. The narrow agenda outlined specific legislation to monitor and lobby on, such as appropriations for the National Institutes of Health or allowing more access to physical therapy for stroke survivors.

Second, they established an overall timeline, based on both their interests as well as the congressional schedule. Congress makes funding decisions every year, which determined some of the answers to the question of when they want this to happen.

Answering the questions of who needs to make the decision or where does it need to happen will establish the venue in which you'll operate (see Chapter 4 for more strategies on answering these questions). In the case of the National Stroke Association, Congress makes the decision and, within Congress, the relevant committees are in charge. Your ability to move forward depends on the decision makers' support, so you better make sure you know who they are.

Measurable

You'll notice that the kinds of questions you'll need to answer when developing specific goals are concrete and objective. You can measure what, when, and where by action, time and space, or location. In other words, you know whether what you want has been achieved by whether the action has been taken. You can look at a calendar to figure out if it's taken place within your time frame. And the answer to the "Where will the decision be made?" or "Who will make the decision?" questions are usually pretty clear (although there are nuances that we discuss further in Chapter 4).

This makes these goals measurable. You can look at any time to see if they're being achieved. It may help to use the following formula to create a measurable goal:

I/we will achieve (specific what) by (when). I/we will approach (who/where) to succeed.

For the National Stroke Association, the statement of the specific and measurable goal would be: "The National Stroke Association will increase funds for the National Institute of Neurological Diseases and Stroke from less than 1 percent of the overall National Institutes of Health budget to X% percent. We will achieve this goal by 2014 and will need to approach the U.S. Congress, specifically members of the House and Senate Appropriations Committees, to succeed."

Remember, this statement should stay in your head. Chapter 8 will offer additional insights into crafting a more sophisticated message that will resonate with your audience.

Attainable and/or Achievable

You've probably heard the self-help maxim "Your attitude, not your aptitude, will determine your altitude," attributed to Zig Ziglar. The idea is that what you can achieve is limited only by your personal perspective. So if that's true, why would you need to choose attainable goals? If you have the right mind-set, isn't every goal attainable?

In truth, many goals are attainable through hard work, perseverance, the acquisition of necessary skills, and luck. But the external environment (over which you may have very little control) can play a huge role as well.

In Washington, D.C., this is usually a matter of how the political party in control of the government (or parts of the government) feels about your particular cause. President Barack Obama pushed hard for health care and financial services reform in the first two years of his presidency (2009-2010) in part because both the House and the Senate were controlled by Democrats. He was aware of the fact that this status might change in the next election—and it did. Health care and financial services reform of the scope and intent enacted in 2010 would have been impossible after Republicans took over the House in 2011.

You'll need to ask yourself if the goal you're reaching for can be attained given the external environment. Potentially mitigating environmental factors may include overall economic issues, what the opposition is up to, or even the personal views of the decision maker you're targeting. Tactic 6 "Identify the Competition" in Chapter 3 and Tactic 16 "Know What Gets Them Up in the Morning—and Keeps Them Up at Night" in Chapter 5, offer more advice on analyzing the environment surrounding your influence situation.

Realistic

Frankly, I always thought that attainable meant the same thing as realistic, so this SMART criterion confused me. Different people think of it in different ways, but I tend to connect the word *realistic* to a personal willingness and/or ability to achieve the goal. In other words, it's less about what's achievable through the external environment and more about what steps you can take, and are willing to take, to make it happen.

Using the National Stroke Association as an example again, the *R* in their SMART goal centered on their ability to create a broad grassroots network. Knowing that legislators would find it difficult to support increased or even reprogrammed spending in tough economic times, the National Stroke Association worked on their internal ability to create change. Within a year, the organization went from 0 to nearly 5,000 advocates nationwide, all ready and willing to take action. With that level of fire power, the likelihood that they would be heard—and agreed with—increased exponentially. Most important, they focused their effort on the most realistic options for what could be done to move their cause forward. They didn't have the resources to hire pricey lobbyists. Instead, they turned to their more than 60,000 partners in the stroke community to start building the network of citizen advocates.

Timely

We all know that nothing focuses the mind like a deadline, even in Washington, D.C., where decisions are made at the last possible minute. For evidence of this, look no further than recent debates over raising the debt ceiling. As you may know from the news coverage of the issue, the U.S. government often borrows money to fulfill its obligations. The difference between what the federal government takes in every year and what it spends is called the deficit. This amount has ranged from $1.3 to $1.4 trillion in recent years. The cumulative amount that the United States owes lenders is called the debt, and that amount is now more than $15 trillion.

Sometimes the federal government needs an increase in its credit limit or it won't be able to meet obligations. It's kind of like when you max out your credit cards but still need or want to buy stuff. That's when the debt ceiling (or in the case of your credit cards the credit limit) needs to be raised.

Increasing the amount of money that can be borrowed doesn't go over so well with fiscally conservative legislators. However, the debt ceiling problem is exacerbated by the fact that Congress frequently needs the additional funds to cover costs for programs like social security and Medicare. It's hard to say no to sick senior citizens.

The issue came to a showdown in August 2011 when conservative members of the House of Representatives (buoyed by support from special interests dedicated to reducing government spending) decided to make a point about fiscal responsibility. They insisted that any agreement to raise the ceiling include specific and binding steps for making cuts in federal programs.

On August 2, 2011, the decision got down to the wire. In fact, the government was within a couple hours of default. Finally legislators reached a deal that favored the more fiscally conservative members. It's clear they would never have achieved their goals without this deadline.

Deciding that you will achieve such-and-such goal *someday* rarely gives you the drive you need to get off your rear end and do something. So your SMART goal should include a specific and realistic time for accomplishment. This deadline can depend on external pressures (as it did in the debt ceiling example), or it can be set according to your own internal time frame or some combination. Either way, being time-bound improves your chances of success.

Specific Takeaways

If you take away any lessons from this tactic they should be:

- Make your goal *specific* by knowing:
  - What you want, both on a general level (e.g., I want *x* dollars of new business) and on a very specific level (e.g., I want this particular customer, who will supply approximately *x* dollars in revenue.)
  - When you want it, in terms of both your timeline and your audience's
  - Who can give it to you
- Make your goal *measurable* by establishing yard sticks or benchmarks for success.

- Make your goal *attainable* by factoring in the potential impacts of external factors (such as the economy).

- Make your goal *realistic* in terms of what you're willing or able to do to achieve it.

- Make your goal *timely* by knowing what external deadlines exist or by setting your own deadlines.

Tactic 4: Know Why You Want What You Want (and Why Your Audience Might Want What You Want)

I learned about this all-important tactic when talking to a congressional staff person during deliberations over the breakup of the Bell Telephone monopoly. For those unfamiliar with this issue, let me give you some background. In the dark ages before cell phones, one company (AT&T) enjoyed a government-sanctioned monopoly over almost all long-distance and local telephone service. Those initially supporting the construct (approved in the late 1930s) argued that it provided an incentive to build the nation's telecommunications network, which it certainly did. There's nothing like guaranteed income to promote investment.

By the 1970s, federal courts decided that the monopoly had grown to the point where it violated antitrust laws. In other words, it had served its purpose in building the nation's infrastructure and now served only to limit free enterprise. In 1982 AT&T divested into seven regional companies, known as the baby bells.

As a result of this ruling, as well as growing pressure from potential competitors, Congress began deliberations to allow more companies to provide telephone services. Legislators reasoned that new business models, such as those associated with cable television companies, could provide continued investment in the nation's infrastructure while at the same time promoting free enterprise. These efforts resulted in a series of bills, including the Telecommunication Act of 1996.

I became involved in all this when working for a lobbying firm representing a large cable company. The company wanted to ensure that these legislative efforts would serve to promote or, at a minimum, not stymie their efforts to provide services (and, of course, make money).

Naturally, a significant part of the strategy focused on meetings with key congressional staff, in which I participated. We crafted SMART goals, had specific asks, and did everything we could think of to make the issue relevant and interesting to the various offices. I remember that in one of the first meetings, after we'd very carefully explained all this to the staff person, she said, "Great. Why do you want that?" Unfortunately, my first thought was "Uhhh . . . because our client wants to make more money."

This was not a good answer.

It was no secret that our client wanted more money. Asking for a meeting on behalf of a cable interest in their district clued the legislator's office into that fact. What the people in that congressional office really wanted to know was why *they* should want what we wanted or, at a minimum, why our ask might do others in their district some good.

In this case, arguments about the benefits of competition, opportunities for job creation, and increased access to telephone services got to the heart of why the decision makers should care. In addition, some legislators were interested in the idea of promoting smaller business interests by breaking up a large corporate entity. Still others distrusted monopolies and sought every opportunity to reduce their impact on the economy.

To succeed, we needed to put the argument in the context of why they should want what we wanted—because it would benefit citizen or business interests in their district. Fortunately, more experienced lobbyists in our firm developed those messages. Once we did that, we were far more successful in getting the message across.

Specific Takeaways

If you take away any lessons from this tactic they should be:

- Be clear on your own reasons for wanting what you want (i.e., your self-interest).

- Think about the reasons why your audience should want what you want. It's usually not just because you want it.

- Know enough about the decision maker to identify the best possible reasons for his or her interest. See Chapter 5 on knowing your audience for more advice on this issue.

Tactic 5: Know What You're Talking About

Polls show that Americans believe foreign aid programs make up about 21 percent of the federal budget.[1]

When asked what they thought an appropriate amount to spend on foreign aid programs would be, they said 10 percent.

In fact, foreign aid programs comprise less than 1 percent of the federal budget. Yet many people would call, write, or visit our congressional office and suggest that funding for foreign aid programs should be reduced to provide financing for their pet project. In essence, they had no idea what they were talking about.

Granted, no one expects the general citizenry to understand all the details of the complicated federal budget process, and we were always happy to provide more details or explanation. However, even

---

[1]http://www.pbs.org/newshour/rundown/2011/03/foreign-aid-facing-proposed-cuts-public-perception-problem.html

those who should have known better frustrated us with their lack of understanding. I saw this with an organization who contacted us regarding their interest in preserving funds for a Forest Service program. In one of his proposed budgets, President Bill Clinton slated the program for elimination. This group raised a great hue and cry, contacting congressional offices left and right and demanding an immediate fix to the problem. They believed that cuts were imminent and inevitable without congressional action.

Although they were registered lobbyists, they clearly did not know much about the federal budget process. The proposal they were freaking out about really wasn't going anywhere. Every year the president submits a proposed budget to Congress that has no force of law and, in many cases, is completely ignored by the congressional leadership.

Sure, it's important to stay on top of issues as they come up. However, this group spent a lot of time and political capital on a nonissue because they did not understand the basics of the process. The effective interests knew enough to help us help them, without wasting our time explaining away problems that did not exist.

If you're going to be outraged about something, make sure you know what you're outraged about. The same is true for wild enthusiasm. It's not enough to say, "Gee, this is great." You've got to know why it's great—and why others would think it's great as well.

Specific Takeaways

If you take away any lessons from this tactic they should be:

- Thoroughly research your problem and/or solutions—not just from your perspective, but from the perspective of the decision maker as well.
- Be prepared to say, "I don't know but I'll get back to you" and then do it.

Applying the Know What You Want Rule in the Real World

Let's look at the common goal of wanting to find a job. That seems like a pretty clear goal. But what kind of job? By when? At what salary? Where do you want to be physically located? If you say, "I want to find a job," you are not being very specific. If you say, "Within the next six months I will find a job in sales for an IT company located 20 miles from my house," you are specifying what you want.

To meet the criterion that your goal be measurable, you'll need to know what yardstick you'll use to measure progress. It may be something as simple as defining whether you have a job or you don't. Or you might want to add in step-by-step measurements. Will it be number of resumes submitted? Interviews conducted? Ads responded to?

Is your goal attainable given the external environment? In an economic downturn it might be difficult to get a job in a short period of time, or at a particularly high salary. Or, using the example above, if you're more than 20 miles from the nearest city, you're probably not going to get a job much closer.

In terms of being realistic, you'll need a positive mind-set to undertake that hard work, persist through the tough times, and acquire the necessary skills. You'll also need a clear-eyed assessment of your own willingness and ability to take action. Too many people have a goal of getting a job and then never send out resumes or make phone calls. That's not very realistic.

Finally, you'll want to be timely by setting a specific and realistic deadline for your goal. What external or internal factors will impact your ability to get a job in six months? Do you have a deadline you must meet—like when your savings will run out? Or perhaps, for younger readers, when your parents will insist you move out of their house?

Once you're clear on your SMART goal, figure out the why behind it. Your self-interested reason for your ask is usually pretty clear. It's no secret to a potential client or employer, for example, that you'd like a sale or a job. Being honest with the decision maker about that upfront generally helps your cause. Successful influencers take this a step further by figuring out why the decision maker might be interested. They are then well prepared to answer the "Why do you want that?" question without resorting to the obvious.

The "Why do you want that?" question might be phrased differently depending on your ask. For example, if you want to make a sale, the prospect may say, "Why should we go with you?" If you answer, "Because our company wants to make money," you probably wouldn't be very influential. An answer of, "Because we want *your* company to make money and here's how our service can help," would probably better help your cause.

Finally, be sure you know what you're talking about. Isn't it frustrating when you talk to a salesperson who knows nothing about his or her own product? I experienced this recently when trying to contract with a service for providing online webinars. My basic questions such as "Can we record the presentations?" and "How does the registration process work?" were for the most part met with, "Well, I'm not sure but I'm sure it will work for you" or "Gee, that's a good question." These responses did not instill a great deal of confidence.

Don't be that salesperson (or job applicant or house buyer or whatever). Before you present a problem or a proposed solution to someone please know what you're talking about. At a minimum, if someone asks you a question you don't know the answer to, it's totally appropriate to say, "I don't know, but I'll get back to you." And then get back to the person. Quickly.

Chapter 5 provides additional ideas on how to research your audience to help prepare you for any questions you may get.

Chapter 3

Know the Competition

Concentrate your strengths against your competitor's relative weaknesses.

—**Paul Gaugin**

Who would oppose legislation to provide the children of military service members with a lapel pin? Or to authorize the Internal Revenue Service to make an apology payment to a taxpayer for an action that has caused the taxpayer excess expense or undue burden? Or the National Childhood Brain Tumor Prevention Network Act? Yet none of these bills have seen the light of day, not because people think they're bad ideas (perhaps unnecessary) but because they are competing with thousands of other legislative ideas for resources, particularly in terms of time and energy.

Given how hard it is to move forward on even seemingly innocuous or good ideas, imagine the difficulty of persuading someone to support you when it comes to something really controversial, like health care reform or right to life/choice issues. Clearly every cause faces some sort of obstacle. It might be competition, opposition, or just the difficulty, as outlined in the preceding examples, of capturing someone's attention. Without some level of conflict, everyone would agree with you pretty quickly and there would be no influence game for you to win or lose.

You won't succeed unless you identify the obstacle and learn more about the reasoning behind it. You'll also want to know what arguments your opponents will use against you, their likely strategies, and what tactics you can best use in response. Tactics 6 through 11, outlined in this chapter, will prepare you for anything the other side has to dish up.

Tactic 6: Identify the Competition

Start with the simple step of identifying the competition. Who stands to lose if you get what you want? Who stands to gain if you don't? The potential losers could be external, like another company or organization. If you are trying to sell a product or service, for example, outside businesses compete with you. Those seeking that dream job will find other applicants to be a threat. Similarly, members of Congress find that they will compete with other legislators for the committee or floor time to fully consider a piece of legislation.

You might also face internal competition, like another department. Internal competitors may be a bigger threat, because your opponents are as familiar with the decision maker as you are and may have more powerful allies. They may keep you from increasing or even maintaining your department's budget, or from getting upper management to see things your way. A government relations office for an association or company, for example, often competes with other divisions, such as membership or conference services, to maintain its budget. The government relations team usually has a more difficult time making its case, because the benefits to the organization as a whole are less tangible.

This internal competition can come even from the audience you're trying to influence. At our firm, we find that some of our biggest competition comes from the potential clients themselves. They almost always believe they would be able to do the things we would do for them. Recognizing that, we make sure when marketing our services to mention the stress-reducing benefits of what we do. Sure, the clients themselves could try to monitor legislation or schedule meetings, but it would likely cost them more in the long run, increase their workload, and be less effective. We'll never convince them they can't do it, but we may be able to convince them that their time would be better spent on more productive and less stressful activities.

In addition to identifying the potential losers, Washington, D.C., lobbyists figure out ahead of time what other groups may benefit from their specific policy or funding ask. As discussed further in Tactics 10, 11 and 22, these groups can serve either as competitors or allies. Either way, lobbyists take time to know what or who they're facing and plan accordingly.

Specific Takeaways

If you take away any lessons from this tactic they should be:

- Know that every influence situation faces some obstacle. Otherwise there would be no need to persuade anyone to see things your way.
- Figure out who will lose if you succeed and who will win if you don't.
- Figure out whether your competition is external, internal, or both.

Tactic 7: Know What You're Competing For

Just because you have competition does not mean you'll be locked in a battle to the death. Sometimes your opposition might feel very strongly about the issue, but most of the time you're contending for the same limited time, attention, or money. In Washington, D.C., although most conflicts seem to be about a basic principle or the ideological high ground, what they're really about is resources.

Resources

Many people lobbying the federal government want money or, as it's sometimes euphemistically called, resources. They might want actual cash, or they might want an increase in funding for a beneficial program or a policy change that will help them make more money or not lose money. Business interests, for example, lobby against the so-called death tax, also known as the estate tax. (The tax is named such because the federal tax code requires a payment of 35 percent of estates valued over $5 million when a business is turned over to family after the death of the owner.)

At the same time, these businesses may lobby for research and development tax credits. The anti–estate tax cause would decrease the amount of cash coming in to the government. The pro–research and development cause would increase the amount going out. Overall, these businesses are simply looking for an allocation of resources favoring them. It's not necessarily bad—it's just how it is.

Even the most altruistic causes—protecting the environment, curing a specific disease, or saving homeless puppies (a favorite of mine)—look for government support. Your first response may be that these are handouts, until you realize that some of these handouts support programs like cleaning up hazardous waste in your neighborhood (e.g., the federal Superfund program), finding a cure for cancer (e.g., the National Institutes of Health), or federal law enforcement against puppy mill businesses.

Regardless of how you feel about government handouts, each of these special interests seeks to influence the distribution or collection of resources. And each competes with the other for an ever-decreasing level of resources. Those who win in this environment recognize that there are many good causes, and their good cause competes with everyone else's.

Time and Attention

Time and attention are valuable commodities as well. Members of Congress have hundreds of people asking for meetings every week. Those requests, paired with votes, committee hearings, party meetings and campaign activities make for a very busy schedule. Committee leaders have difficulties carving out time as well. In 2011 alone, the House Ways and Means Committee, for example, had more than 800 bill referrals. This means that before the bill referred could move through the rest of the process, that specific committee would have to approve it. There's just no way to consider all of those proposals. Those that do move forward have strong advocacy and lobbying campaigns behind them, led by special interests who understand that the fiercest competition is for attention.

The Ideological High Ground

All that said, the ideological high ground is one of the favorite competition fields in Washington, although in truth, many politicians really see it as tool to help them win the race for time, money, and attention.

What is the ideological high ground? Former presidential candidate Michele Bachmann found her high ground when Congress debated the very important issue of compact fluorescent lightbulbs in 2011. At issue was a Bush administration policy designed to save energy by requiring manufacturers to develop more energy-efficient varieties of lightbulbs. Although the policy was supported by both industry groups and environmentalists, Congresswoman Bachmann managed to bring the House of Representatives to a standstill in her efforts to stop its implementation. She argued that the government should have no role in determining lightbulb use, saying, "I think Thomas Edison did a pretty patriotic thing for this country by inventing the lightbulb. And I think that if you want to buy Thomas Edison's wonderful invention, you should be able to!" Tea Party activists and others interested in smaller government applauded her efforts and the issue became symbolic of the overall concerns about the reach of government (somewhat ironically, because the initial policy came from the Bush administration, small-government proponents).

Business groups like the National Electrical Manufacturers Association (NEMA) joined environmental and consumer advocates in arguing for the consumer, environmental, and economic benefits of the policy. They pointed out that no one would be forced to buy any particular type of lightbulb, but to no avail. Representative Bachmann had captured the ideological high ground, at least for the time being. In fact, a budget bill passed in December, 2011 specifically prohibited the Department of Energy from spending money on implementation of the fluorescent bulb policy until October 2012— a victory for the anti-fluorescent bulb forces.

In fact, capturing the ideological high ground can help you win other battles over the competition, so think carefully about whether you can do so.

Finally, recognize that you may find others who support your cause for entirely different ideological reasons than you do. Several patient advocacy groups, for example, support increasing eligibility for physical therapy services under Medicare. Though they may represent different constituencies, such as stroke versus cancer survivors or even those who provide physical therapy, they all want to see people have more access. Yet they may still compete for time or money (both finite resources), because they will always look at any issues through the prism of their own interest. They want this issue to succeed for their own reasons, and will always put those reasons front and center. In other words, sometimes very like-minded groups may seek the same ideological high ground as you. You must decide whether joining forces will help you get there. See Tactic 11 on circling the wagons for more details.

Specific Takeaways

If you take away any lessons from this tactic they should be:

- Find out what you're competing for. Sometimes it's not what you think.

- Figure out whether your opposition is truly opposed or just trying to get the same time and attention you are.

- Where possible, capture the ideological high ground. It can help you win time and attention (and sometimes money). Chapter 8 outlines strategies for crafting an effective message.

Tactic 8: Research the Opposition

Lobbyists know the opposition inside and out. When the opposition includes a member or members of Congress, lobbyists will know what bills they have introduced, what votes they have taken, and what statements they have made concerning the issue at hand. They know the percentage by which they won their last election and who contributed to their campaign. They know who works for them now and who worked for them in the past. They even know where they grew up, where they went to school, and their favorite hobbies. It all may sound a little creepy, but knowing the opposition helps both structure and strengthen your argument.

To find the answers to these questions, special interests conduct opposition research. This process involves identifying the weaknesses of those who may oppose you, whether it's a specific opponent in an election or someone who disagrees with your policy position. To do the same in the "real world," once you've identified who your competitors are and what you're competing with them for (as outlined in Tactics 6 and 7), you'll want to answer the following questions about their connections, interests, and general background on the issue.

- Have they ever expressed an opinion on your cause or issues related to your cause? If so, what?

- What issues do they talk about, even if unrelated to your own? Knowing that will help you understand where they might start the attack. For example, a special interest opposed by an organization like the American Civil Liberties Union (ACLU) can usually safely assume that the first attacks they'll have to respond to will be related to Constitutional rights, such as freedom of speech. This is because the ACLU sees itself as the "guardian of liberty," and specifically these rights. So if they are going to oppose you on something, that's their "go to" argument.

- Do they have any key supporters? While in the nation's capital we might figure this out by discovering who contributed to their campaign. Elsewhere, you might be able to find out whether your competition knows the decision maker you're trying to reach, or knows anyone who knows that person.

- Who are their key opponents? You know the saying "The enemy of my enemy is my friend"? Although this has been described in the past as a Chinese or Arab proverb, I wouldn't be surprised to discover that it had originally been espoused by a Washington, D.C., special interest. It's always a good idea to find and cultivate those who may also have an interest in seeing your competitors fail.

- What outlets do they use for delivering their side of the story? When you know where their arguments might be aired, you may be able to offer an early rebuttal. In addition, knowing their favorite outlets will help you know what aspects of an issue most interest them or what side they're likely to come at you from. In the lobbying world, knowing that an opponent uses Fox News as opposed to MSNBC to deliver a message will tell you a great deal about that opponent's general perspective.

Knowing all this will help you achieve one of the most important goals in effective influence: know where your opposition *will be,* not where they are.

The analogy that helps me understand this principle relates to my efforts to learn underwater photography skills (stick with me here. I swear this is relevant). I'm an avid scuba diver and really wanted to take beautiful pictures of the underwater world I love so much. However, I was wholly unsuccessful, mainly because I took pictures of where the fish was, not where it was going to be. I never really learned how to figure out where the fish would be going, but I did learn how to apply this tactic to influence efforts in Washington, D.C.

Specific Takeaways

If you take away any lessons from this tactic they should be:

- Knowing who the opposition is and what you're competing for is not enough. You must know enough about them to be prepared ahead of time for the kinds of arguments they will put forth.

- Your opposition has a view of the world that you must understand to succeed.

- Your opposition's view can be determined through an understanding of their previous statements on your cause, their general topics of interest, who their supporters and opponents are, and what outlets they use for delivering their side of the story.

- Know where your opposition will be, not where they are.

Tactic 9: Research Yourself as if *You* Were the Opposition

One of the more overlooked aspects of opposition research is figuring out what your opposition will say about you. But that's not all you need to know. To be successful you have to discover your *own* weaknesses—and be prepared to confront any arguments made against you.

Public radio and television stations and programmers apply this tactic to their advantage in their ongoing fight against cuts to funding for the Corporation for Public Broadcasting (CPB). Many institutional factors negatively impact the public broadcasting community's ability to advocate effectively. First is "cultural": I can tell you that in my experiences as a government relations staff person for NPR, direct lobbying of elected officials, in addition to directly violating federal regulations, run counter to a culture deeply concerned about maintaining journalistic integrity. It's tough to report without bias on federal policy issues when embroiled in a bitter debate over a federal legislative action.

In addition, the dispersion of the public broadcasting system makes it difficult to develop and deliver a coordinated message. In the context of recent funding battles, the fact that more than 900 radio stations and 350 television stations around the country benefit from federal funds certainly assisted public broadcasting's lobbyists, and allowed access (on the basis of constituency) to almost all 435 members of the U.S. House of Representatives and all 100 Senators. Nevertheless, getting all of these stations (or as many as were interested) on the same page presented an extremely challenging obstacle.

Finally, public broadcasting leaders recognized that most decision makers, even their supporters, understood very little about public broadcasting's funding stream. Opponents often argued that organizations like NPR and the Public Broadcasting Service (PBS) should produce programming without federal dollars. In reality, the vast majority of federal funds go directly to local stations, not to the programmers. Local stations use those funds, in addition to those acquired from other sources, to purchase programs from sources like NPR, PBS, and other national programmers. That's how national organizations like NPR and PBS make money.

That may seem like a distinction without a difference, but it was an important factor in how the public broadcasters played the influence game. Their first challenge was to get decision makers to understand that cuts in federal dollars directly and negatively impacted stations in that legislator's district. Only after that fact was clear could they make arguments for preserving funding.

These strategies proved very successful. In fact, Congressman Earl Blumenauer (D-OR) identified the efforts to protect funding for public broadcasting in the fiscal year 2011 budget as one of the most effective lobbying campaigns he's seen in recent years. Neither the Corporation for Public Broadcasting nor the Ready to Learn program, which funds public television programming and services for kids, saw any cuts. They succeeded in part because they knew their weaknesses and addressed them in developing their campaign plan.

Take some time to answer the questions outlined in Tactic 8, and think about how they relate to you and your cause. What weaknesses will your opponents discover? And how can you combat them? For example, if you're applying for a job, what will potential employers find amiss on your résumé? Jumping from job to job? A period of

61

Know the Competition

time without employment? Be prepared to explain that openly and honestly.

Specific Takeaways

If you take away any lessons from this tactic they should be:

- Recognize that if your opponents know what they're doing, they will be ferreting out your weaknesses.
- Research your own issue and background to find those weaknesses.
- Prepare to address those weaknesses should they arise.

Tactic 10: Divide and Conquer

To stop something from moving forward, Washington, D.C., lobbyists often engage in a practice known as divide and conquer. When your opponent consists of a coalition of groups, the other side's lobbying strength will be diminished whenever these groups can be splintered.

For example, in 1993, then Representative Marjorie Margolies-Mezvinsky (D-PA) walked down to the well of the House of Representatives and cast her vote for a controversial tax on British thermal units, or BTUs. The chamber rang with chants from the other side of the aisle of "Bye-bye Marjorie." Opposed by the energy industry, House Democrats nevertheless pushed the bill through only to have it die an ignoble death in the Senate. With her vote Representative Margolies-Mezvinsky sealed her fate—a fate shared by 33 other Democrats—as an incumbent who lost her seat in the next election cycle.

House Democratic leadership and President Clinton calculated, incorrectly as it turns out, that the BTU tax could be spun as a vote to raise revenue and balance the budget, not a vote for new taxes. The Senate Republican leadership, on the other hand, made it clear they would never support a new tax (buoyed by the no-new-taxes pledge of then president George H. W. Bush).

People in Washington, D.C., say that the energy industry helped the Senate overpower the House. In fact, the tactic become so popular that it morphed into its own verb, as in "to 'BTU'" the other side. The industry's lobbying strategy was to divide and conquer the two chambers—and they did so with a vengeance. They used circumstances and differing political philosophies to break up coalitions and stop the tax. Perhaps more important, that one vote played a significant role in the subsequent Republican takeover of the House, which happened in the next election. It was the first time in more than 40 years that the Republicans had gained control of the House of Representatives—and although this might not all be attributable to that one vote, it can certainly be argued that the divide and conquer strategy dramatically impacted the shape of American politics for years to come.

Specific Takeaways

If you take away any lessons from this tactic they should be:

- Know who supports the opposition.
- Figure out the varying degrees of support: are they with the opposition to the death or a little squishy?
- Try to peel off the less enthusiastic in order to move you toward your goal.

Tactic 11: Circle the Wagons

After all these Machiavellian perspectives on the competition, it may surprise you to know that sometimes it makes sense to work with the competition. You may seek to solve a mutual problem—and then plan to fight out the particulars in subsequent battles.

The National Alliance of Public Transportation Advocates (NAPTA) took this approach during congressional debates over funding for surface transportation programs in 2004. These discussions often turn into a battle between those supporting roads and those supporting buses, trains, subways, and the like. Different groups support public transportation for different reasons, such as promoting cleaner air, increasing access to jobs for low-income communities, promoting community development, and reducing overall traffic congestion. Federal public transportation programs provide separate funding for each of these different aspects of public transportation and, for the most part, these groups all compete with one another for those resources.

However, when it came to going up against organizations lobbying for a larger part of the overall transportation pie, the public transportation groups came together to form NAPTA, an umbrella organization dedicated to simply increasing the pool of dollars dedicated to public transportation. Every message focused on an overall increase in dollars: squabbles about how those dollars would be spent happened outside NAPTA. As an organization, NAPTA lobbied only for increased public transportation funding, period.

In this case, although different groups competed for smaller parts of the pie, leaders of the cause recognized that the much bigger battle was for overall funding for public transportation. Although it was a tricky balance to achieve, they managed to circle the wagons around the larger question. In the end, they recognized that it's much better to argue over a larger pie.

In fact, business interests circle the wagons frequently when they form together into trade associations. Washington, D.C., abounds with groups made up of individual companies that compete with each other all the time, but come together in the face of larger policy issues.

Specific Takeaways

If you take away any lessons from this tactic they should be:

- Figure out if there's a larger battle you should be fighting, and whether your natural competitors may turn out to be allies.

- Find one common theme for the larger battle that everyone can agree to.

- Give coalition members the flexibility to argue on the smaller questions.

Applying the Know the Competition Rule in the Real World

To truly understand the competition, start by understanding who else wants what you want. You'll likely think of the external competitors first but remember that sometimes your biggest challenges come from the inside. Those internal competitors may come from your own organization or they may be within the organization you're trying to influence. The important thing is to know who they are.

Next you'll want to know why those competitors may think you should not have what you want. Often, it's because they want it themselves, but there also may be entirely different reasons, like they believe they don't need your service and can save money or time without it. Think of these as opponents instead of competitors. Either way, you'll want to know what arguments they will make against you. What weaknesses will they find, and how might they use those weaknesses?

Finally, consider the tactics of either dividing and conquering your opponents or circling the wagons on your side. Either approach will help you peel off members of the opposition and move forward on getting to yes.

Chapter 4

Know the Arena

The place where the system and people's intentions meet is the political arena.

—Peter Garrett

People ask decision makers for inappropriate things all the time, and congressional offices are no exception. Misdirected requests I encountered when working on Capitol Hill included everything from "We need a stop light in our neighborhood" (a local decision) to "The municipal court should waive my parking tickets" (a judiciary-related decision) and even "The Internal Revenue Service should stop auditing me" (a federal agency decision, or sometimes a law enforcement decision). One of our constituents even asked us to move a post office closer to their business so it would generate more foot traffic for them. I gave them very high points for creativity.

Likewise, people often go to Congress to change policies enacted by federal agencies and vice versa, not understanding that federal agencies and Congress play two entirely different roles in the policymaking process. Congress makes laws; agencies implement them. Therefore, asking an individual member of Congress to change an agency decision makes no sense. Sure, members of Congress can certainly make agency officials nervous. And they can certainly work to pass legislation prohibiting a rule's implementation. But they cannot unilaterally change agency decisions, no matter what they promise on a campaign trail.

Each of these examples had at least one thing in common: the person asking wasted a lot of time talking to the wrong people in the wrong decision-making arena. A couple of them were also impractical, unethical, and illegal.

You won't get what you want if you don't know who can give it to you. If you want a job, you need to know who has openings. If you want to sell something, you need to know who is buying. This seems pretty obvious, but way too many people figure out their goal and then hope someone will come out of the woodwork saying, "Yeah, that's a good idea, let's do that." In fact, many self-help gurus tout what I refer to as the Ready, Fire, Aim approach as a means of achieving overall success. They argue that worrying incessantly about taking what's considered the "right" action prevents us from doing anything. In other words, it promotes internal paralysis.

In the influence game, however, it makes no sense to spend all your resources in the wrong decision-making arena. You must aim the messages about what you want to the person or people who can actually give it to you. Your entire strategy—building internal support, creating messages that resonate, effective message delivery, follow-up—builds upon your understanding of the arena and audience. If you do not know the arena and the players you won't get ahead, period.

Tactic 12: Find Your Decision Maker

As noted previously, Congress passes laws. Federal agencies implement laws. The federal court system (including the Supreme Court) interprets laws. Although you must identify the institution associated with your goal, you'll also need to find those people within the institution that will make the decisions. For example, Congress as an institution passes laws, but people vote on them. Influencers in Washington, D.C., find the right people.

Sometimes the powerful people you might expect to be in charge, such as committee chairs and ranking members (i.e., those in charge of the various committees), are the first stop for legislative initiatives. They, along with the overall leadership of the House and Senate, wield significant power over both the content of bills and the timing of when they will be considered. Members of certain committees, like House Ways and Means, Senate Finance or the House and Senate Appropriations Committees, hold more sway over the outcome of money bills than others. Individual House members have less power to impact legislation than individual members of the Senate. In fact, the list of power structures within the organization go on and on. Effective lobbyists know that it's essential to have not only a general sense of who might be influential, but to understand these nuances as well.

Special interests build their lobbying campaigns by moving from power decision maker to power decision maker as their issue progresses. They also know that sometimes the decision maker is not who others say it is or even who they think it's supposed to be. On paper, it may seem that Vice President So-and-So is making the hiring decision or that Manager Such-and-Such takes the lead on purchasing. That person may not, however, be the true decision maker. Your job is to ferret out who that true decision maker is—and sweet talk him or her.

Sometimes that person may even be lower on the totem pole than your on-paper audience. Here's a not very well kept secret from Washington, D.C.: in general, members of Congress do not make all the decisions in their office. With schedules that include 20 to 30 meetings per day and hundreds of votes on every issue from funding federal programs to clean air laws to whether to name a post office after Elvis, members of Congress rely on their staff for day-to-day decisions. These might include questions like whether to sign on to a letter supporting (or opposing) a policy proposal, whether to schedule a particular meeting, or what the legislator should say to constituents regarding his or her political perspectives.

Every congressional office structures its decision-making process around the preferences of the legislator and the types of decisions to be made. For example, in most offices the scheduler exercises a great deal of control over who gets to meet with the legislator. Communications and press requests will be referred to the press secretary. Other staff help shape the legislator's perspective on different policy issues. Most political questions go to the chief of staff. Even the staff assistant at the front desk wields significant power. This person decides who will get White House tour tickets and will go to great lengths to track them down in the vast congressional ticket black market (yes, it really exists).

In short, lobbyists and special interests take the time to find the real go-to people in the office. Then, as discussed further in Tactic 16, they figure out what makes them (and their boss) tick.

Specific Takeaways

If you take away any lessons from this tactic they should be:

- Target your effort toward one or more specific decision makers.
- Sometimes those decision makers aren't who you think they might be, or who they appear to be on paper.
- Often, the true decision makers will be lower, not higher, on the totem pole.
- Never assume that the person answering the phone has nothing to do with your decision. Sometimes he or she is the most critical person to impress.

Tactic 13: Find Your Plan B (and Plan C and Plan D) Decision Maker

Policymakers arrive at decisions through a long and winding path that changes often and in surprising ways. There's often more than one way to achieve your goal, and more than one audience to approach. Tactic 44 discusses creating alternative plans for success in more detail. For now we'll look at finding all the different decision makers who can get you to your goal.

The National Association of Exclusive Buyer Agents (NAEBA) often looks to several different policymakers to achieve their policy goals. NAEBA members are exclusive buyer agents, or those who represent only buyers in a real estate transaction. They have slightly different interests than traditional real estate agents because they always work to get the buyer the best deal, not the seller. Ralph Nader helped found the organization, so as you can imagine they have a pretty strong pro-consumer bent.

One of their goals is to increase agency disclosure, or the initial disclosure to anyone involved in a real estate transaction, of who represents whom. It's always good for a buyer to know, for example, that the very nice realtor he or she met at an open house represents the seller.

There are many ways to promote agency disclosure. You could attack the issue in all 50 states. You could work with Congress to introduce legislation mandating or encouraging disclosure. You could work with federal agencies to promote disclosure on federal mortgage forms.

NAEBA, a client of ours whom I lobbied for from 2009 to 2011, decided to take a multipronged approach based on the political environment. In 2009, when Democrats were in control of the Congress, we sought a stand-alone legislative fix and worked with a Democratic legislator interested in promoting the consumer aspects of the issue. When Republicans came to power with an agenda that included housing reform, we connected the issue to that effort. We turned to federal officials implementing rules on consumer protection to see if something could be done there. In 2012, a NAEBA board member worked with champions in the Maryland General Assembly to have model state legislation introduced in that venue. Outside the direct political system, leaders of the organization built alliances with consumer groups, business interests, and even traditional realtors.

Basically, NAEBA leaders assessed the political environment and found their Plan B, Plan C, and Plan D decision makers. Though the issue of agency disclosure has not yet been resolved, NAEBA has their strategies in place to take advantage of any opportunity that comes their way.

Specific Takeaways

If you take away any lessons from this tactic they should be:

- Sometimes there are multiple paths to your goal.

- Assess the environment in which you're operating and imagine different circumstances. What if the economic outlook shifts? Or if there's a change in leadership? How would your plan change in those situations?

- Prepare for those circumstances by planning ahead. Identify the many different ways in which your goals can be achieved and find the relevant decision makers.

- Be ready to take advantage of any breaks you may get.

Tactic 14: Ask the *and Next* Question

As a young congressional staff person (actually, very young—I hate to break it to you, but our government is being run in large part by 20-year-olds), I was assigned the responsibility of developing a piece of legislation regarding the transfer of nuclear waste through state and local jurisdictions. We were opposed to having highly radioactive materials transported through our district, which would have been likely had efforts to move waste to a centralized location been successful.

Unfortunately, a proposal to simply ban the shipment of these materials through our congressional district would never have flown. No one else in Congress cared enough about our district to support such a bill—and would likely be concerned that, if such a bill were to pass, the waste might wind up trekking through their area. In addition, the bill would face Constitutional challenges for violating the interstate commerce clause. If you have better things to do than read the Constitution every day word-for-word, I'll tell you that the interstate commerce clause basically states that Congress may not make any laws that restrict commerce between states.

We got around these issues by proposing something a little sneakier. Rather than suggesting that no waste could go through our district, we suggested that all jurisdictions could decide whether they wanted to accept the transport of waste through their area. Ingenious, right?

Proud to have come up with that idea, I skipped (figuratively, not actually) over to an office known as legislative counsel and asked them to draft a bill to do just that. The legislative counsel's office is filled with really smart people who know the U.S. legal code inside and out. Whenever one of the 20-year-olds on Capitol Hill needs someone to turn brilliant ideas into legislation, they work with legislative counsel. These smart people dotted all the *i*s, crossed all the *t*s, and turned my beautiful idea into a piece of legislation that my boss promptly introduced.

Here's where I screwed up. I never asked what would happen after the bill was introduced. I knew that the first step on its journey was the Parliamentarian's office, where it would be referred to a specific committee for consideration or, in this case, *four* different committees. It's hard enough to get a bill through one committee—a referral to four committees spells disaster.

This happened because I did not ask the *and next* question over and over and over again until I understood the whole process. It would have been possible to easily change some of the wording to limit referrals. But I didn't know that because I didn't ask. What happens after drafting the bill? And next? And next? And next? The *and next* question can make or break your influence effort.

Specific Takeaways

If you take away any lessons from this tactic they should be:

- Understand as much as you can about the process associated with your influence situation before delving in.
- Assess the risks and opportunities of each step you take by asking yourself and others the *and next* question.
- Know as much as you can about what will spell disaster for your cause—and make sure to avoid these things!

Tactic 15: Know the Rules of the Game

Remember the *Schoolhouse Rock* cartoon on how a bill becomes a law (or am I showing my age)? People in a community identified a problem (it was the need for a railroad crossing, as I recall), went to the congressman who represented that area, and asked him to propose a law. The congressman sat down at his typewriter, typed up a proposal, and submitted it for consideration.

Then both a subcommittee and a full committee had to have hearings, the bill had to be considered by the entire House, and then the same thing happened all over again in the Senate. Even if passed by both chambers, the bill's journey continued, as the House and Senate had to resolve any differences and send the proposed law to the president for his signature or veto. And don't get me started on what happens if the Supreme Court gets hold of it.

Besides the image of the congressman sitting down at his typewriter, the *Schoolhouse Rock* scenario describes the process very well. No wonder that bill was so happy to become a law!

D.C. insiders know the many details of how this game works. The U.S. House of Representatives, for example, operates under a series of complicated rules and codes for the consideration of legislation. This approach is necessary because, with 435 members of the House, it's nearly impossible to get everyone to agree. So rules have been established to try to ensure a fair fight between the majority and minority (although many argue, on both sides, that the fight isn't always fair).

As you might imagine, this makes the members of the House Rules Committee, which determines the rules of the game, very powerful. In fact, they are so powerful that the party that controls the House always stacks the ratio of the committee in their favor (usually 9 majority to 4 minority) just to be sure that they will always win when it comes to votes within that committee. So anyone seeking to influence that chamber would do well to build relationships with members of the Rules Committee and help their champions use that committee process to their advantage. For example, if you can't get a stand-alone bill considered, you may be able to convince the Rules Committee to allow it as an amendment to another bill being considered on the floor.

The Senate, on the other hand, operates on a principle called unanimous consent. This means that any Senator can hold up a bill and demand certain changes. Senators do this by threatening to filibuster a bill, meaning that they will talk and talk and talk, never relinquishing the floor for the consideration of other bills. You may have heard of some filibusters where senators read the phone book on the Senate floor. The whole goal is to prevent substantive debate until that senator (or group of senators) gets what he or she wants.

Politicians also use rules to circumvent the other side. Leaders in the House of Representatives (no matter which party is in control) set up situations where legislators can vote no on a rule for floor debate without voting on the substance of the bill itself. The legislators can go back to their constituents and say, "I never voted against such-and-such policy," even if they voted against the rule that would have allowed them to consider such-and-such policy. This may seem like one of those "sneaky things politicians do." I'm not condoning it and you may decide that you don't want to "sink to that level." I'm just pointing out that it works.

The difference between the rules and the unanimous consent environments, as well as the use of rules to shoot down the competition, are just two of the many different things a lobbyist or special interest needs to know before developing a strategy. In the real world, this translates into knowing the entire procedure behind your influence situation. For example, if you're applying for a job, when will hiring decisions be made? How can candidates approach those doing the hiring? Are there deadlines for materials? How will decisions be made? Is it a joint decision? A vote? Just one person deciding?

Likewise, if you're seeking a new customer, how do they make purchasing decisions? Does it go through several departments? Do multiple people have to sign off? Is there a cost/benefit comparison that needs to be done? Are there deadlines? The answers to these and other questions about the rules will keep you ahead of the competition (or at least not booted out of the game).

Specific Takeaways

If you take away any lessons from this tactic they should be:

- Every influence situation operates under different rules. You must adhere to these rules to avoid being kicked out of the game.

- Take time to learn both the written and unwritten rules. Beyond the outlined procedure, are there other considerations? How does the culture of the influence situation impact how the rules will be applied?

- Remember that the competition must adhere to the rules as well. Sometimes you can use your knowledge of the rules to circumvent them, or even to win outright.

Applying the Know the Arena Rule in the Real World

Spending all your time talking to someone totally unrelated to your ask wastes both your time and theirs. That's why once you've figured out what you want, one of your first tasks should be to find out who can get you that. That person isn't always the person you at first think it may be, and sometimes that person is lower down on the totem pole than you might imagine. In congressional offices, he or she might even be an 18 year old intern or even a 14 to 15 year old page, particularly if they are the children of friends of the legislator.

At the same time, most goals can be achieved in more than one way. Don't wait until everything is falling apart to figure out Plan B (and C and D). You simply won't have time to prepare yourself and your surrogates (see Chapter 6) to switch gears to your new arena quickly enough. Ask yourself, "What would happen if my Plan A decision maker was no longer around? Who would step in? Do I know that person? Are there other people within the organization (or outside of it) who can get me what I want in a different way?" In my business, for example, every year we lay out different scenarios for reaching our revenue goals. Each approach depends upon our success in a slightly different marketplace. If we find that one area is not doing as well as we thought, we turn to another to fill the gaps. And the worst that can happen from being so prepared? We get more business in all our areas.

Once you've identified the arena in which you're operating, you'll need to learn a whole lot about the rules of engagement there. One way to do that is to ask the *and next* question repeatedly until you understand the entire process. Once you've submitted a proposal, what happens next? And after that? And after that? That process will give you a good sense of the rules of the game, and remember that the person who best knows the rules has a better chance of winning.

Having that background on your cause's environment will prepare you for the next step, knowing your audience (i.e., the influencers).

Chapter 5

Know Your Primary Audience— The "Influencees"

Lead the audience by the nose to the thought.

—Laurence Olivier

In D.C., successful lobbyists never start a conversation with, "What policy issues most interest the congressman?" Nor do they ask, "Has the congressman taken a position on this issue in the past?" If they don't know the answers to these kinds of questions before talking to the congressman or staff person, they are not worth the hundreds (or sometimes thousands) of dollars they get paid per hour.

It is not the decision maker's job to tell you why he or she might be interested in what you have to sell. Finding the answer to that question is your job. If you really want to make that sale, you must walk a mile in another man's Gucci's. Or you could walk a mile in another woman's expensive high heels, but I do not recommend it: the Capitol's marble floors are not easy to navigate in heels.

The influence game is all about knowing how to make the person you're trying to influence feel like your idea is his or her idea. To get to that point, you must be able to see the world through that person's eyes, body, and mind. Most important, you must find all this out (or as much as you can), before your initial contact.

Take the infamous example of the Alaska project that became known as the Bridge to Nowhere. By way of background, one provision in a bill called SAFETEA-LU (the Safe, Accountable, Flexible, Efficient Transportation Equity Act: A Legacy for Users) called for the building of the Gravina Island Bridge in Alaska. It turns out that the bridge would have benefited only 50 Alaskans (and approximately 200,000 annual airline passengers) at a cost of $398 million. It would have been nearly as long as the Golden Gate Bridge and taller than the Brooklyn Bridge. It also turns out the chair of the relevant congressional committee, Representative Don Young, was from Alaska. The bridge never did get built, however, because then governor Sarah Palin cancelled the project.

A perfect example of that so-called pork spending they're always talking about, right? But if you think about it, Congressman Young's self-interest dictated that he should help his constituents and the tourists that helped boost the Alaskan economy get from point A to point B without having to resort to an airplane. His constituents, and his desire to help them, were more important than any other considerations. Sure, it may not have been the best use of federal funds, but in a representative democracy individual members of Congress are there to represent the views of their constituents, not everyone in the nation. Anyone seeking to succeed in gaining support for any federal policy, whether a "bridge to nowhere" or increasing domestic oil reserves by opening the Arctic National Wildlife Refuge to oil drilling, voters would need to see the world from *his* perspective, specifically how the policy would benefit them.

Perhaps he went a bit far, though, in titling part of the legislation with the acronym LU because his wife's name was Lu. Sweet, but maybe a little over the top.

So what do we need to know about the audience? Tactics 16 through 18 will show you the best ways to answer this question.

Tactic 16: Know What Gets Them Up in the Morning— and Keeps Them Up at Night

The phrase "Yes, I see your point, but . . ." is not something you often hear in Washington, D.C., especially when one proceeds to explain why that perspective is horribly misguided. Effective lobbyists say, "Yes, I see your point *and* . . . " Then they proceed to explain why that point relates to something in the legislator's self-interest. This might be something like keeping their job or maintaining their budget. From a more altruistic perspective a legislator's self-interest may revolve around moving forward on their policy agenda or even a wholly unrelated interest, like a favorite charity or hobby. The policy agenda, charity, or hobby will get a politician up in the morning, whereas the question of reelection keeps him or her up at night. Most of the time, unless you're dealing with a legislator in a very safe seat (meaning he or she faces relatively little opposition in elections), these factors are equally important.

For Congressman Mike Kreidler, for whom I worked as a legislative assistant from 1992-1993, the issue that got him up in the morning was health care. As a former optometrist he was keenly interested in efforts to improve America's health care system (even as far back as then!). It was the guiding principle of his work in the office. He introduced 25 bills, 25 percent of which were related to health care. Anyone who could connect their issue with health care would be heard in our office. Over a decade later on connection with the 2008-2009 health care reform debate, Bradford Fitch of the Congressional Management Foundation made this same point saying, "Those special interests lobbying on provisions of the health care bill that succeeded did so because they connected with the policymaker's interests."

The best lobbyists know before they even walk in the legislator's door what most interests that legislator, and then they talk about that. If the legislator has introduced bills on the environment, they find the environmental aspects of their argument. If it's technology, they talk about high-tech stuff. They key is that they've figured out what the legislator likes, not just what interests the lobbyist. Usually they can find that out by looking at the bills they've introduced and reading their biographies.

In addition, as Judy Schneider of the Congressional Research Service (CRS) points out, effective lobbyists know what the legislator sees as the next stepping stone in his or her career. For example, one of my old bosses really, really wanted to get on the Ways and Means Committee. This is a very exclusive committee in the House of Representatives that oversees tax and revenue laws. To demonstrate his interest in the policy issues, and his potential usefulness to committee members, he spent years introducing tax-related legislation. This helped him show his knowledge of the issues as well as his political acumen in achieving their passage. Lobbyists who came to him with tax-related proposals generally got at least a hearing—and sometimes his support.

The best way to find out their thoughts on the next stepping stone is to look at their actions. Members of the House of Representatives start paying a whole lot more attention to the rest of the state when they decide to run for the Senate. Senators become more visible nationwide when they run for the presidency. These actions speak louder than words.

Finally, sometimes the thing that gets them out of bed in the morning *literally* gets them out of bed in the morning. Representative Earl Blumenauer (D-OR) runs almost every morning and has completed several marathons. During my initial job interview he asked me what I thought of a running meeting. I thought he asked what I thought of running a meeting. But no, he really wanted to know what I thought about having a policy discussion while going out for a jog. Frankly, I didn't really have an opinion on that as it had never come up, but we worked it out (although I discovered that it's hard to take notes and, well, breathe, when talking while running). In fact, his dedication inspired me to run (okay, jog—and sometimes walk) two marathons.

The point is that if you're an avid runner, you can probably meet with Earl Blumenauer. It will have to be at 5:00 AM with your jogging shoes, but believe me, his staff will thank you.

On the flip side is what keeps them up at night. The two biggest concerns with legislators are keeping their job (through reelection) and maintaining budgets.

In terms of reelection, we can talk about lobbyists, special interests, money, and corruption in the political process all we want, but what it all ultimately boils down to is that every elected official needs to convince voters that he or she is worthy of reelection. The voters are really the ones who hire (or fire) legislators.

Members of Congress will lose their seat if they do not receive at least 50 percent plus one of the votes on Election Day. To get there, they need assistance with gathering both funds and volunteers to run a campaign. Knowing this, successful special interests often employ a combination of what are known as grassroots and political action committee (PAC) strategies to help get those legislators who understand and agree with their perspectives elected. Grassroots strategies are those that get voters engaged in the decision-making process, and PAC strategies are those that help legislators raise the funds they need to run a campaign. As much as we may not like the role money plays in the political process, it takes $1.1 million to run a House of Representatives campaign these days and $6.5 million to run a Senate campaign. Presidential campaigns cost upwards of $750 million. Those lobbyists and special interests that help provide those resources will likely rise to the top of an elected official's radar screen.

You might also want to consider where your audience's budget comes from when investigating their self-interest. Very rarely will you find a decision maker with completely autonomous control over his or her financing. For the most part, someone else determines the flow of money in and out of the institution or division. Lobbyists understand this basic rule and spend time learning where the money comes from, where it goes and, perhaps most important, who it comes from.

Finally, think about what keeps them up at night in terms of the competition (as discussed in Chapter 3). Dave Wenhold, former president of the American League of Lobbyists and one of the founders of Miller/Wenhold Capitol Strategies, a successful lobbying firm, told me a story of how he managed to land a university as a client.

87

Rather than simply explaining to them the value of his services, he reviewed lobbying disclosure reports to see if any of their competitors had a presence in D.C. Several other universities in the state *did* have professional lobbyists on their side. This state of affairs made Dave's potential client nervous—and he won their business. He landed this client because he figured out what keeps them up at night and then used that information effectively with his audience.

Tactic 18 goes into more detail about finding, categorizing and working with these "influencees." For now, just know that decision makers almost always have keeping their job and sometimes maintaining their budget as priorities.

Specific Takeaways

If you take away any lessons from this tactic they should be:

- Know how the decision maker you're trying to influence got his or her job. Who hired him or her? You may decide to pull those people into your influence effort.

- Know how the decision maker gets and/or maintains his or her budget. Is that a decision made by someone else? If so, who is it, and is that person someone you might want to integrate into your effort?

- Gather as much background information on the decision maker as you can, including what kinds of jobs they've held, where they went to school, what clubs they belong to, their hobbies, even what religion they are. This will give you a good sense of the kinds of issues and people that will matter most to them.

- Use that information to pinpoint what gets your audience out of bed in the morning or keeps them up at night. Is it a particular issue? A charity? A simple desire to make more money?

Whatever it is, you can use that information to track down others who might have some sway over them.

Tactic 17: Know What They Need from You, Not What You Want to Give Them

In one congressional office I was the legislative aide responsible for transportation, environment, energy, small business, campaign finance, animal welfare and, well, a whole bunch of other issues. I know a little bit about everything. I'm wonderful at a cocktail party, but I'm horrible if you want to have a substantive policy-related conversation with me.

I wanted to know three things about the lobbyists I met with: first, their expertise, second, why that expertise mattered to our district and third, where to find them if I needed them. I had no need to know everything they knew—they already knew it, so how would cramming my head full of that information help me? The best lobbyists figured that out. They spent my valuable time (and their very expensive time) on answering those three questions, and were then available when I needed them to tell me more. The worst lobbyists spent a great deal of time and effort writing white papers, crafting talking points, developing backgrounders, and putting together three-hour briefings, when those things were not at all what I needed. In some cases they didn't even know that we already supported them on a particular issue, which made the meetings really easy for me, but not a great use of time for them.

Of course, what's needed in a legislative environment may be different from what's needed in a business or consumer situation. I've responded to enough requests for proposals (RFPs) to know that those making hiring or acquisition decisions may need to justify that with reams and reams of paper (or megabytes). The point is to identify what your audience needs from you and then provide that.

Specific Takeaways

If you take away any lessons from this tactic they should be:

- Focus on what your audience needs from you, not what you want to give them, and spend your time working on that information, not everything else.

- Be sure you know if your audience already has a position on your issue. You'll save valuable time in developing persuasive materials if you don't really need to persuade them.

- Don't spend time with your blinders on regarding your perspective on an issue. See things from the audience's point of view.

Tactic 18: Categorize Your Primary Audience into Champions, Supporters, and the Rank and File

It's frustrating when everyone you talk to says, "Yeah, that's a good idea," or "Yeah, you'd be perfect for that job," or "Yeah, we could really use that product," and yet nothing happens. In Washington, D.C., this is the status quo. Those who are successful in moving from "we support this idea" to "let's get this done" know how to differentiate between champions, supporters, the rank and file, and the opposition.

Find or Develop Champions

On April 13, 2011, Representative Roscoe Bartlett, a Republican from Maryland, introduced House Resolution 1513, the Great Ape Protection and Cost Savings Act. Among other things, the bill called for the prohibition of invasive research on great apes. As the sponsor of the bill, Representative Bartlett became a champion of this issue.

What made him such a powerful champion was the fact that when he was in the Navy he conducted research on chimps.

Notice, too, the specific wording of the title of the bill: the authors quite cleverly realized that in tough economic times, bills related to cost savings may succeed, whereas bills related to saving great apes, though important, are less likely to capture both attention and support. They connected to the issue du jour in D.C., as discussed in more depth in Tactic 34.

Champions will carry the water for your cause. On Capitol Hill, these are the legislators who will introduce the bill, urge other legislators to cosponsor, and nag the House or Senate leadership to move the legislation through the process. Without a champion, even the best policy issues won't go anywhere, not because they aren't good ideas, but because no one is willing to pursue them.

As you're looking for champions, remember that unusual champions trump all others. Because of his relevant experience working with primates, Representative Bartlett's involvement with the Great Ape Protection Act makes a powerful impact on those he must influence to move the legislation forward.

Don't Ignore Your Supporters

Never assume your supporters will support you forever. Sometimes they get weak-kneed and need some shoring up. Or they may simply get consumed with other things and not make your issue a priority. One of the most common phrases you hear in Washington, D.C., is "Well, no one ever asked me to . . ." You can finish that sentence with any number of examples, such as "vote yes" or "cosponsor that bill." Without your constant engagement, supporters can wander off. They may not become opponents, but their lack of active involvement will probably reduce your impact.

Supporters also serve as the pool from which you will find future champions. Legislators retire, lose elections, or sometimes even have to quit in the face of a scandal. Putting all your eggs in one legislative basket rarely makes sense. It makes even less sense in the business world.

Identify the Rank-and-File and then Maintain Their Neutrality

Those who haven't made a decision yet (or are involved in some way, but frankly don't care either way) are the rank and file. As Congressman Earl Blumenauer says, "Sometimes it's not about changing minds. Sometimes it's just about getting the opposition or the neutrals to stay home."

In 2010 those identified as Republicans or independents supporting Republicans turned out in droves at the polls. As a result, Republicans won an additional 63 votes in the House of Representatives to gain a 242-193 vote advantage—and nearly captured the Senate. This success depended in part on the number of Republican-identified voters the party was able to get out to vote. But perhaps more important were efforts to ensure that those who didn't really care stayed away from the polls.

On Capitol Hill, this translates into a strategy of lobbying under the radar. If your policy ask is relatively simple, sometimes it's best to see if you can just slip it into a bill rather than advertising your effort far and wide. In places other than Washington, D.C., sometimes your best strategy is to simply ensure that others don't get involved, especially if you're in a situation where you have a strong champion, several active supporters, and little opposition. In those cases, the more you actively engage others, the more you might generate opposition to your cause.

Identify and Then Marginalize or Co-opt the Opposition

The opposition is just what it sounds like. These decision makers actively don't want you to get what you want. When beginning work on reform of the nation's health care system (Access to Health Care Services for All, or Obama Care, depending on your perspective), one of the first meetings President Barack Obama held was with business interests, including the U.S. Chamber of Commerce, health insurers, and the pharmaceutical industry. He knew that he wouldn't even get out of the starting gate without their support or, at a minimum, their silence.

He made a deal. They agreed to support both a comprehensive bill and specific provisions within that bill that would pay for reform through billions of dollars in cuts to existing programs from which they benefited. In exchange the companies would receive very favorable paybacks, like increased coverage for prescription drugs and, of course, the opportunity to gain millions of new clients through coverage mandates. Some would call it a compromise. Some would call it pandering to the powerful interests. Either way President Obama recognized the politics of the situation and co-opted the opposition from the very beginning.

Specific Takeaways

If you take any lessons away from this tactic they should be:

- Look at the playing field and assess current players in terms of whether they are champions, supporters, rank and file, or opponents. You may find that many of the players are of unknown status.
- Where possible, develop your own champions. They will carry the water for you within the influence arena. Your champions may be those who helped you get your foot in the door.

- Don't ignore your supporters. You don't want them to wander off.

- You don't always need to push your cause. Sometimes it's better to slip quietly under the radar.

- Think about whether you can co-opt the opposition from the outset—or at least along the way.

Applying the Know Your Primary Audience Rule in the Real World

Time and attention are finite resources. You know that as well as anyone in Washington, D.C. You need to figure out how to get your audience to pay attention to you. To do that, you need to know what they already pay attention to, and focus your approach on that.

I think of this in the context of salespeople who call to "learn a little bit more about what our company does" so they can see if the product they're selling would be right for us. Many of the questions they ask are answerable from our website. I really have better uses of my time than to read them text from our website, and I'm sure they do as well.

Knowing your audience also involves knowing what they need from you, not what you want to give them. If they need a 50-page dissertation on the value of your product, give them that. If they need one page, give them that. One way to be sure you're talking your prospect's language is to actually talk their language. In drafting proposals, I sometimes find that using the exact terms they use in the RFP yields results.

Finally, your primary audience can usually be categorized into champion, supporters, rank and file (or unknowns), and opponents. Champions and supporters can make your case. Rank and file or opponents can break it. Figure out who's who and strategize accordingly.

Chapter 6

Find Your Surrogates—The "Influentials"

Everyone has an invisible sign hanging from their neck saying, "Make me feel important." Never forget this message when working with people.

—Margaret Kay Ash (founder of Mary Kay)

Effective lobbyists understand the limits of their effectiveness and look for opportunities to engage surrogates in delivering their message. Believe it or not, the majority of the time this group of influentials includes constituents. In fact, as noted in Chapter 1 on the principles of influence, a recent report from the Congressional Management Foundation found that 97 percent of offices ranked a visit from a constituent as far more influential in the decision-making process than a visit from a registered lobbyist.[1]

Why is this important?

Sometimes you are not the best person to deliver the message. I learned this when working on a local request to fund the purchase of land for a National Scenic Area partially in our district. The member of Congress I worked for at the time had a very strong pro-environment voting record, so the advocates from our district sent a very environment-friendly group to our office. We hugged the trees and we saved the land and all was well.

---

[1] http://congressfoundation.org/projects/communicating-with-congress/perceptions-of-citizen-advocacy-on-capitol-hill

At the same time, they also needed to persuade a very conservative senator from Washington State. Frankly, he was less interested in hugging the trees and more interested in protecting businesses and jobs. So the environmentalists forged an alliance with very conservative farmers in the area who wanted to sell their land near the scenic area and get out, because the environmentalists were driving them crazy. They got the senator on board and won the funding.

No matter which side of the equation you were on, this unholy alliance demonstrated that finding those who will influence your primary audience (and persuading them to take action) makes a difference. The following tactics will show you how.

Tactic 19: Know Who Will Be Positively Impacted

A community group looking to convince local city council members to invest in a skateboard park understood this principle as well. In building their coalition they started with the obvious groups, like skateboarders and local businesses that sell skateboarding equipment. But when they thought a little more about who else might be positively impacted by a skateboard park, they came up with an interesting answer: the local shopping mall. Merchants weren't at all thrilled about the skateboarders in their parking lot and really wanted to encourage them to go somewhere else. The shopping mall management got involved. They recruited people to deliver a message that the skateboard park investment would be good for business and they helped finance the effort. The coalition won and the park was built.

In addition to negative impacts (see Chapter 3 on knowing the opposition), your proposed solution to your cause will likely have a positive impact on someone. Be creative in finding out who that is. You may be able to add them to your arsenal of influencers when the time comes.

Specific Takeaways

If you take away any lessons from this tactic they should be:

- In most cases others will be positively impacted by your cause. Figuring out who they are will help you move forward.

- Create a list of people and organizations likely to be directly impacted by your proposed solution.

- Think creatively about those who may be indirectly but positively impacted.

Tactic 20: Know Who Influences Your Decision Maker

Although you may hold no direct sway over a decision maker, you may know people who do. To find them, take a look at who surrounds the decision maker as well as to whom he or she turns for advice.

Your list may include superiors, staff, friends, or family, and you may be surprised at the number of connections you already have or can build. In Washington, D.C., we call this a 360-degree review or an environmental scan. It's used in part to figure out every possible angle of influence. The nexus between those affected positively by your outcome and those who influence your decision maker the most will form the core of any alliance you may be able to build.

The following categories are a starting point for your own 360-degree review, but be creative! You never know when you'll find just the right influencer.

Superiors

Ultimately, the superiors of any member of Congress are those who elect him or her into office—the voters. At the same time, as discussed briefly in Tactic 12, "Find Your Decision Maker," there is a hierarchy within the House and Senate. Some legislators, like the Speaker of the House or the Majority Leader of the Senate, are voted into leadership positions by their colleagues.

In addition, through hard work and knowledge of issues (and a fair amount of internal lobbying), more senior legislators may become committee chairs or ranking members (i.e., those who are seen as the leaders of the committee for the party not in power). Those in these types of positions wield a significant amount of influence. For rank-and-file members of the House or Senate, it's important to stay on the good side of ranking members and committee chairs. In many ways they are superiors.

Staff

"Aww, man. I thought I was going to meet with the congressman. Instead I have to meet with just you?" Does that sound very influential? Hopefully not, but I heard that at least once per day while working on Capitol Hill. Any lobbyist who uttered those words made a significant mistake at the start of our relationship. They alienated one of the most important people in the decision maker's office.

Most people outside Washington assume that the member of Congress makes all the decisions when it comes to how to vote, what bills to support, and what positions to take when communicating with constituents. Though the end responsibility certainly does rest with the member of Congress, as discussed in Tactic 12, those who work for the congressperson make many of the day-to-day decisions, such as who the legislator should see, what bills they should cosponsor, and how they should vote on noncontroversial issues. Nevertheless, many special interests obsess about meeting the legislator himself or herself. In addition to insulting the staff person when they express this desire, they are wasting time and effort on reaching the member of Congress when they could achieve their goal much more quickly and easily by working with the staff.

As Emily Sheketoff of the American Library Association says, "Be nice to those whom others condescendingly call 'the little people,' such as assistants and interns. Those are the people with a big influence over the policymakers."

Look at this in the light of your own influence situation. Who surrounds and supports the decision maker? For example, does he or she have a personal assistant? If so, this person is essential to your effort. Help them help you by treating them with respect and leaving them with the impression that their boss should meet with you. Who knows? They may become a sort-of lobbyist for you within the office.

Friends

Occasionally, my boss would come into the office from his morning workout and say, "Hey, we should introduce legislation on . . .", and here he would mention some random subject in which he had never expressed an interest before. My first response? "Who were you talking to at the gym this morning, Congressman?" Invariably, it was a friend of his who was interested in this mysterious subject. Moral of the story: friends matter.

Back in the olden days before the Internet, we used to find the friends of elected officials by asking around. Now social media websites provide similar information much more quickly and without anywhere near as much effort. Use sites like LinkedIn or Facebook (also discussed in Tactic 39) to search for a decision maker you're trying to reach. You'll be surprised at how many people in your existing network are associated with the person. Maybe they worked for him or her in the past, or they went to school with them. Imagine the power of being able to reach that person through an existing connection as opposed to making a cold call.

Family

With hundreds of phone calls, e-mails, and letters coming in every day, staff in a congressional office must prioritize their responses to messages. As for me, I replied in the following order: first, the congressperson; second, the congressperson's spouse or child; third, my spouse; fourth, other congressional staff, and, finally, everyone else. Notice that my boss (i.e., my superior who gave me my job) was number one—and his or her spouse was second. I remember one time the daughter of one of the members of Congress for whom I worked called with a so-called emergency. She needed to know how to boil an egg. We answered her question on the spot.

I find this idea of family connections to be particularly useful at the local level. In my training sessions, I'll always ask whether people are personally related to a decision maker (such as a city council member) or know someone who is. Almost every single time someone has said, "Yeah, county commissioner X is my cousin" or "Yeah, one of my board members is married to councilman Y."

We don't always think about these connections because they seem very natural, but it's good to figure that out. Just don't make him or her uncomfortable (see Tactic 43, know the difference between persistence and stalking).

Contributors or Funders

Depending on how cynical you are, it may or may not come as a surprise to hear that those who contribute to a legislator's campaign have some degree of influence over him or her. That said, the political contribution equation is not always the "Hey, I'm giving you money, now you have to listen to me" situation most people envision. In fact, I'd argue that most people contributing to a legislator's campaign already have some level of influence over him or her because they fit one of the other categories that define influencers. They're usually approached to be contributors because they're already in tight with the legislator, not the other way around.

Regardless of whether you believe that or not (I'm guessing most people won't), knowing who contributes to a member of Congress's campaign will tell you a great deal. Think about who might contribute to your own decision maker's organization. If it's a nonprofit group, you probably should be looking at funders. If a business, look at investors. Even if just a department within an organization, look at where the budget comes from (as discussed in Tactic 16, know what keeps them up at night). Money flows in and out of the relevant organization somehow. You'll generally find a pretty influential person behind those funds.

Other Persuasive Interests

In January 2005 several lobbying firms were called out by the *Washington Post* and other publications for making a concerted effort to hire Republican lobbyists. Many in the lobbying and public interest world cried foul. They argued that those belonging to the other party were being discriminated against.

However, the lobbyists on K Street (D.C. shorthand for the section of the city where many lobbyists work) were making smart business decisions. After 40 years of domination by the Democrats, control of the House of Representatives had gone to the Republicans. Overnight those lobbying firms that had built their reputation around their connections to certain legislators were suddenly powerless. To survive, they had to find Republicans—and find them fast.

These new guard lobbyists fall into the category of other persuasive interests because they had connections with legislators that the firms needed. They could get a meeting with the new legislators almost immediately.

There are others outside the beltway who can get these spur of the moment meetings as well, such as opinion leaders in the elected official's district. We call these the *grasstops* because they have access to a legislator or staff person by virtue of their position in the community.

Putting aside lobbyists and grasstops, however, the most successful advocates in Washington, D.C., are plain old constituents. This is why special interests often employ some sort of grassroots strategy to get citizens directly connected with their legislators. Pharmaceutical companies, for example, often work with patient advocacy groups to encourage increased access to drugs that treat certain diseases. They know that as voters, members of these groups have a tremendous amount of sway with legislators.

The National Stroke Association, the Brain Injury Association of America, the National Spinal Cord Injury Association, the United Spinal Association, and United Cerebral Palsy employ this strategy in partnering with Allergan on the Open Arms: Raising Awareness of Upper Limb Spasticity campaign associated with increasing access to Botox. Many patients have found relief with this drug, which is generally associated with preserving the facial features of Hollywood celebrities. Telling the story of the actual therapeutic uses of this drug from the patient perspective makes the message much more persuasive.

Specific Takeaways

If you take away any lessons from this tactic they should be:

- Successful special interests create and cultivate a pool of influencers that surround the decision maker.
- Figure out who the decision maker interacts with on a daily basis and who they turn to when making decisions. These may include superiors, staff, friends, family, funders, and the catch-all category of other persuasive interests.

- These influentials serve as third-party validators for the worthiness of your cause. This is why the gathering of referrals is such a useful tactic in sales. People trust other people more than they trust the person who will directly benefit.

- Find your most powerful potential allies by cross-matching who will be positively impacted (Tactic 19) with those who influence your decision maker. You'll want to devote time and effort to that more targeted group of influencers.

Tactic 21: Don't Network—Netplay

Lobbyists always want to know who you work for. They're not so interested in where you work, or even what kind of work you do. They focus on the *who* because they know that everyone they meet may eventually serve a purpose toward attaining their end goal. That sounds crass, I know. But take heart in knowing that the best lobbyists take this one step further and find out how they can help the other person attain *their* goal. Effective networking, like effective lobbying, is a two-way street.

To be honest, I hate the term *networking,* and I'm not fond of the idea, put forth by many, that it is a complicated procedure. Lobbyists network all the time and they do not follow a 20-step process for getting to know people. I prefer to refer to what happens in Washington, D.C., as *netplaying.* It's not a chore; it's something special interests enjoy.

In Washington, D.C., there are two kinds of netplaying—depth and breadth. Breadth netplaying is when you go to events and meet people who may, at some point in the future, be useful. Depth netplaying is when you identify who you specifically want to meet, find out where they hang out, and go there. Both kinds of netplaying are important to successful influence efforts.

Perhaps most important, relationships built through netplaying should last beyond the other person's usefulness to you. As noted in Chapter 1, in the early 1990s I had the misfortune to lose my job when my boss lost his bid for reelection. What I lovingly referred to as my personal unemployment problem came at a difficult time for people associated with my political party. There had been a change in leadership on Capitol Hill, which meant that no one wanted to hire any members of the party not in power.

That's why it surprised me when I received a condolence call from the managing partner of the law firm where I had previously worked as a legislative assistant. In D.C. terms I was no longer important. I didn't work for a member of Congress, nor was it clear I ever would again. In short, there was no reason to believe that I would be of any use in the future. Yet a very busy lobbyist took the time to call me and ask whether he could be of any use. I never forgot that phone call, and when I did get another job on Capitol Hill, you better believe that lobbyist was always welcome in our office.

This concept of netplaying serves me in the real world as well. As a small-business owner I find that my client contacts within an organization will change. Sometimes when the person I know leaves I'm faced with the problem of reselling the new person on our service. However, I can have some control over the outcome by proactively building relationships with others in the organization.

Finally, the most successful netplaying tactics involve developing positive relationships with people you really like. Sure, you may have to work with some challenging types to achieve your goals. But I find that my most gratifying influence successes grow out of the friendships I've built in D.C.

Specific Takeaways

If you take away any lessons from this tactic they should be:

- Who you know may make or break your influence effort, so work to build relationships that will serve you well in the future.

- Don't look at networking as work. That almost never yields the kinds of relationships you need to succeed. Think of it as netplaying.

- Breadth netplaying is the practice of meeting people at events and staying in touch, recognizing that at some point in the future they may be willing to help you.

- Depth netplaying is the practice of finding out who might be most influential with your audience (see Tactic 20) and finding opportunities to meet them.

- Both breadth and depth netplaying tactics are necessary to move you toward your goal.

- Netplaying is a two-way street. Those who are most successful at it find mutual benefits. In short, they don't just "use" others.

Tactic 22: Partner with Polar Opposites

When the Humane Society of the United States (HSUS) sought to pass legislation changing the treatment of egg-laying hens, you'd think the last group they would partner with would be the United Egg Producers (UEP). After all, the HSUS strongly criticized the UEP for the egg industry's treatment of these animals. They accused some in the egg industry of cruelty for keeping hens in very tight cages.

Yet in July of 2011 these two groups came together in a historic agreement to advocate for tougher federal standards for the treatment of all 280 million hens involved in U.S. egg production. They agreed to seek introduction of legislation to change labeling laws, create larger caging environments, and ban certain inhumane practices.

Many supporters of the HSUS are vegan (i.e., they eat no meat, poultry, fish, eggs, or dairy products). The egg producers clearly are not. As an interest group and an industry representative they have very different end goals. The HSUS seeks to protect animals—as they see it. The egg producers seek to provide a quality product at a fair price to American consumers. Yet they found common ground on a legislative proposal that, if passed, would achieve a win-win for both sides, even though it would cost egg farmers $4 billion to implement the new housing systems over 18 years, according to a spokesman for UEP.

These opposites-attract coalitions reduce controversy—a sought-after result in Washington, D.C. If two diametrically opposed groups can come to agreement, the thinking goes, their proposed initiative must make sense for everyone. Representative Ted Poe (R-TX) and Representative Earl Blumenauer (D-OR) took this approach when joining forces to introduce House Resolution 3658, the Water for the World Act of 2012. The bill seeks to strengthen U.S. foreign assistance in water and sanitation for some of the world's poorest countries. Because these two congressmen vote against each other the vast majority of the time, their agreement on this issue leaves the impression that their bill must be very reasonable, or at least not controversial.

In partnering with those most likely to disagree with you, you leave your audience with the impression that what you have to propose makes so much sense, even polar opposites can agree.

Specific Takeaways

If you take away any lessons from this tactic they should be:

- In addition to looking for partners who are generally on the same page, look for those who are polar opposites. In some cases they may agree to be with you on a particular issue.

- Remember that partnering with polar opposites helps reduce controversy.

- When you reduce controversy, you make it easier for the decision maker to agree with you.

Tactic 23: Remain Civil, Even with Those You Really Don't Like

As noted in the previous tactic on polar opposites, in Washington, D.C., it is not uncommon for a person to disagree vehemently with someone on one issue—and then agree with that same person wholeheartedly on another issue. Take the example of the Cooperative Alliance for Refuge Enhancement (CARE), a coalition that includes conservation, recreation (including sportsmen), scientific, and wildlife organizations to fight for stronger refuge systems and funding. One issue brought these disparate groups, including crunchy, green environmentalists and far more conservative sportsmen, together— wildlife preservation. They disagree on most policy issues, yet sought the same outcome, albeit for different reasons. One group believed in protecting the environment and wildlife for their own sake. The other believed in protecting the environment and wildlife so, frankly, they could hunt them.

These groups understand the importance of building bridges, not burning them. The American Public Transportation Association (APTA) and the American Association of State Highway and Transportation Officials (AASHTO) used this tactic to their advantage during recent debates over funding for roads and public transit. In most situations, these two groups fight tooth and nail for the finite resources available for surface transportation programs. However, when Congress undertook a major overhaul of transportation programs in 2005, these two groups joined forces to both fend off attempts to raid their

109

dedicated trust fund and to advocate for the highest level of funding possible. This alliance held even while they argued at the same time, in the same venue, with the same players about how that money should be divided.

The interpersonal bridges built by these groups have civility as their foundation, which is why every contact you have with any decision maker, potential ally, or even enemy should remain as courteous as possible. Believe it or not, even members of Congress abide by the civility rule. When making public statements they refer to each other as "the gentle lady from California" or "the gentleman from New York," even if the next words out of their mouth are ". . . is totally and completely wrong."

That's why it was big news in Washington, D.C., when Representative Allen West (R-FL) referred to Representative Debbie Wasserman Schultz (D-FL) as "vile, despicable, and cowardly" as well as "not a lady" during a dustup over spending caps and the Medicare budget. Not only was it not exactly nice, but he completely violated Capitol Hill's unspoken civility rules. His comments were in response to her statement that "[t]he gentleman from Florida, who represents thousands of Medicare beneficiaries, as do I, is supportive of this plan that would increase costs for Medicare beneficiaries. Unbelievable from a member from south Florida." Ironically, Wasserman Schultz maintained the civility code by referring to West as the "gentleman from Florida," even while blasting his position on the issue.

Some considered West's comments to reflect the extreme partisanship (accompanied by extreme nastiness) that surrounded the issue. In the end, it certainly didn't help West's cause and now the two representatives have difficulty working together to benefit their region of the country.

All that said about playing nice with others, some people are absolutely toxic. This is as true for the political world as it is for the real world. There's even an annual survey run by *Roll Call,* known as the newspaper of Capitol Hill, rating the likability of members of Congress. Year after year the same legislators show up on the top of the list of the unliked. Not only are these individuals bad for moving forward a policy issue, it's no fun to work with them. For your own influence situation you'll want to figure out who these people are and avoid them. Just don't be rude while doing it.

Specific Takeaways

If you take away any lessons from this tactic they should be:

- Even when you disagree with someone on one issue, you can agree with him or her on another.
- Build bridges, don't burn them.
- Live by the civility rule—you never know when you'll need to work with your opposition in the future.
- Avoid toxic people.

Applying the Find Your Surrogates Rule in the Real World

Imagine the power of having someone very influential with your audience putting your cause in front of him or her. Finding those people and cultivating relationships with them often makes far more sense than spending all your time trying to get to the decision maker, especially when you don't already know that person well.

Think about who the inside influencers are for the decision maker you are trying to reach. To find them, conduct a 360-degree review of that decision maker and his or her position to identify those who hired that person, those who provide funding for their department, or those who work for that person. For example, if you're looking at this in the context of a business or hiring decision, take a look at the management structure of the company, including the board members, as well as any staff who may work for the person you're trying to reach.

In some cases, these influentials may be your polar opposite. These are valuable partners in an influence situation because they reduce controversy. Perhaps most important, as you're finding these influentials, remain civil, even if they drive you crazy. You never know when you may want to work with them in the future.

Chapter 7

The Campaign Plan

Before beginning, plan carefully.

—Marcus Tullius Cicero

You've probably realized that with all this research and thinking you really haven't *done* anything yet. You haven't barged into the decision maker's office and demanded to be seen. You haven't talked to other people about what it is you want. Everything you've done so far is behind the scenes.

Now's the time to put everything we've done so far to use and create that strategy that will help you move all these good ideas forward.

Planning a campaign sounds simple: get the right people in the right place with the right message at the right time. That's easier said than done. Not only do you need to find the right people, determine the right place, and craft the perfect message, you'll need to inspire action, both from your surrogates and from yourself. That's what the campaign plan helps you achieve by providing a structured strategy for moving forward. These tactics will show you how.

Tactic 24: Don't Bring a Knife to a Gunfight (or a Screwdriver to a Nut and Bolt)

Effective lobbyists and special interests use more than direct meetings with members of Congress to achieve their goals. All government relations efforts are built on a variety of tactics, including public

115

relations, grassroots, grasstops, direct lobbying, and campaign contribution strategies. Lobbyists pick and choose which strategies match the depth and breadth of their effort.

For example, you can't go up against tobacco interests with nothing but a wish, a prayer, and sad stories. That's why savvy special interests like the Campaign for Tobacco-Free Kids use public relations, lobbying, grassroots, and judicial strategies, among others, to succeed in battles against the $80 billion tobacco industry. The Campaign led the coalition that help craft the Family Smoking Prevention and Tobacco Control Act, which became law in 2009 over the strong objections of tobacco interests.

Likewise, in the business world, you can't expect to triumph over a much larger, more financially impressive company with nothing more than a can-do attitude. Although it's true that you can and often should start with just one person (you!), you'll need to take steps to grow the effort into something more comprehensive.

In addition to making sure the power of your tools matches that of the opposition's, remember that different tools have different uses (or at least that's what I'm told by people who know how to use tools). Successful lobbyists develop a range of effective influence tools and then figure out what will work best in which situation. In the government affairs world, these tools may include direct outreach to members of Congress from professionals (i.e., lobbying), public relations, engaging citizens through grassroots strategies, and/or engaging in a campaign contribution strategy that builds strong relationships with existing or new legislators. In most cases, an effective lobbying effort will involve all of these tools to some degree.

For example, if you're introducing a very new issue or very new group to members of Congress, a public relations campaign designed to raise the profile of the issue and generate positive buzz may be the best approach. On the other hand, the passage of a very esoteric tax provision will require a more targeted and expertise-based approach.

The Academy of Managed Care Pharmacy (AMCP), a national professional association representing the interests of the pharmacist profession associated with managed care, uses a range of different tools to achieve their goals. They mainly used direct lobbying strategies (i.e., professional lobbyists meeting directly with legislators and their staff) during the national debate on health care reform. This tool worked for them because of the technical nature of their issues and the fact that frankly no one knows who they are. Their more depth versus breadth approach made more sense because both their desired policy outcomes and their audience were limited.

However, as implementation of the health care law shifted to the state level, AMCP leadership knew they would need to focus on this battleground, but at the same time recognized that developing direct lobbying resources in each of the 50 states simply wasn't very realistic. Instead, they focused on creating grassroots structures in each state led by a member volunteer coordinator. The state-level grassroots effort also serves to build capacity for future national efforts, as individual AMCP members build the skills necessary to impact the policy environment at both the state and federal levels.

Applying this tactic in your own influence situation ties back to understanding the scope of your cause, as discussed in Tactic 2, "Know the Nature of What You're Selling." Once you've figured out how extensive the effort will be, you'll be able to choose campaign strategies that match your goals.

Specific Takeaways

If you take away any lessons from this tactic they should be:

- Understand the scope of what you're trying to do and build a strategy accordingly.

- Where possible, match the power of your tools to the opposition's. David and Goliath battles can certainly be won, but they are very difficult.

- Be sure the tools you use match the influence situation. Do you need a breadth approach or a depth approach? Your research about the audience, the issue, the arena, and the influential people will help make that determination.

Tactic 25: Create an Influence Reserve

As mentioned in other chapters, the American Public Transportation Association (APTA), representing the interests of more than 1,500 transit agencies and associated businesses across the country, sees public transportation as a good use of federal transportation dollars. Some policymakers—especially those most interested in reducing the size of government or those in rural areas with less need for public transportation services—disagree. That's why when conservatives captured the House of Representatives after the 2010 election, many observers were concerned about the future of transit funding.

However, the lobbyists at APTA very wisely—and very early on—recognized the benefits of taking a nonpartisan approach. Even in the years when those who were considered their friends were in charge of the Congress, they cultivated relationships with more conservative and anti–big government forces. These relationships served them well, particularly when it came time to make pro–public transportation arguments to a skeptical group of legislators. As a result, at a time when most programs were being cut, Congress increased overall funding for the Federal Transit Administration by 3 percent. Though it's true that some transit-related programs were cut and, of course, public transit advocates believe funding levels are way out of line with real needs, the hits could have been significantly worse.

In short, APTA created an influence reserve. They looked ahead to a time when congressional offices would be less receptive to their traditional allies and found potential influentials for different political times.

In addition to creating a people-oriented influence reserve, consider whether you need a resource-oriented one as well. Sometimes you may need to engage in an all-hands-on-deck effort, but if you do that every time, you may expend all your time, money, and energy too early. In addition, your partners will begin to get tired of your cause and may move on. In Washington, D.C., we call this advocate fatigue, and special interests avoid it by picking and choosing which battles they fight as well as how fiercely they'll fight them.

Specific Takeaways

If you take away any lessons from this tactic they should be:

- Look ahead to when your environment may change.
- Find and engage potential influentials for that different environment.
- Pick and choose your battles as well as the level of your engagement so you can maintain a resource reserve for the future.

Tactic 26: Don't Be a Nigerian Prince

When you check your e-mail (or your old-fashioned postal mail, for that matter), what messages do you notice first? Those communications clearly sent to everyone and their mother? The missives from Nigerian princes eager to hand over a large sum of money in exchange for your bank account number? Or the personalized communications from someone you know? If you're anything like the rest of us, it's probably that last group that captures your attention: personalized, quality communications matter.

Decision makers, even in our nation's capital, are just like the rest of us. They pay more attention to tailored communications, less attention to form communications, and zero attention to spam. Congressional offices consider and respond to communications through a type of triage system by prioritizing messages along the following lines, from least influential to most.

First, completely irrelevant automated communications are the Nigerian prince missives of the lobbying world. Generally these take the form of petitions, postcards, or blast e-mails with identical messages from people who do not live in the legislator's district. In most cases, a computer program tosses these into a virtual trash bin (or an intern tosses them into a real trash bin). I call this point-and-click democracy. Simply clicking a button to express your outrage about homeless puppies or taxes or even health care reform does not make you an engaged citizen. Your communications must have at least some semblance of personal thought behind them to begin to be influential.

The business-world version of this type of communication is a "Dear sir/madam" letter or e-mail advertising a product or service for which the recipient has absolutely no use whatsoever, or which is otherwise clearly not at all relevant. For example, because my husband's last name is Silva, we receive marketing materials in Spanish very frequently in our household, through both phone calls and snail mail. No one in our house speaks any Spanish. These materials go directly into our actual or psychic recycling bin.

The second least effective way to influence a member of Congress is to be a constituent sending a form communication. Don't get me wrong: anything from a constituent is valued in a congressional office. At least these messages are from someone who is relevant to the legislator, as opposed to the Nigerian prince missives. As a constituent, that sender basically hires (or fires) the legislator, and hence holds significant sway (as discussed further in Tactic 20.)

But let's face it, blast e-mails that all say the same thing do not convey a tremendous sense of urgency or, frankly, caring on the part of the sender. In D.C. there's a saying that these types of messages are "weighed, not considered." They may generate a check mark on a form, but they rarely directly influence the decision-making process in a legislator's office. The staff assistant counts up how many form postcards or e-mails or carrier pigeons there are and gives someone higher up an approximate number.

Outside of Washington, D.C., these types of less-than-influential communications are those that advertise a product or service that may actually interest you but are pretty clearly mass messages. When was the last time you received a letter from a credit card company and ran around the house saying "Yay! This credit card company wants me!" Even if you want a credit card, the approach does not generate a feeling of personal interest in you on the part of the company.

Or take the example of cover letters for job applications. Those that are at least properly addressed and specify the job in which the applicant is interested may receive slightly more attention, although it's pretty clear all potential employers are receiving the same text.

Where form communications are second, direct communications from professional lobbyists are third on the list. You'd think this category would be higher up in terms of effective influence potential, but, according to research done by the Congressional Management Foundation (mentioned in Chapters 1 and 6), professional lobbyists don't always hold as much direct sway as people believe. I say direct sway because the smart lobbyists know how to influence through others. They've figured out that constituents have the most power with legislators and work to facilitate direct constituent outreach, instead of undertaking their own.

I can say I've experienced this firsthand. As a lobbyist for a small trade association, I brought in a constituent to meet with the staff of his legislators. They rolled out the red carpet for him, spent time learning about the issues he raised, and made it clear they appreciated the opportunity to meet with him. When it came time for me to go back to the office to ask for help on the policy issue we were discussing, however, they made it clear that they wanted to hear directly from the constituent. My job became less about dealing with the legislator's office and more about working with the constituent to help him deliver the message.

The messages that rise to the top of the influence hierarchy are those communications from someone highly influential that are specific, personalized, relevant, and timely (per the SPIT rule, discussed in Tactic 38). Frankly, these are few and far between. All the members of Congress I worked for asked us to weed through the thousands of communications we'd get in a week to find the 10 or so most personalized and thoughtful letters. Some weeks it was hard to find 10 that met those criteria. The vast majority were form communications and many of the remaining were threatening or from people with limited mental acuity, shall we say.

I'm not going to lie: sometimes (perhaps most of the time) people craft deeply personalized communications about an issue near and dear to their heart and receive nonpersonalized responses about a completely unrelated topic. Clearly that's frustrating because it feels like the person on the other end isn't listening. The best way to manage this situation is to put aside the frustration and write back. Point out the error and ask, politely but firmly, what the decision maker really thinks about the issue. Most people dealing with a lot of mail, e-mail, or phone calls have a system for keeping track of who's already received a form response. With your next communication their initial reaction will likely be, "Oh crap, I can't send the form letter again. I'll have to actually think about what they have to say." This is the response you're looking for.

Your job in your own influence situation is to figure out the communication triage system for the decision maker you are targeting and to avoid sending those Nigerian prince–style messages. For example, you're not going to get very far in influencing a legislator's office by trying to send an e-mail to a catchall info inbox. In fact, it's impossible to send an e-mail through the legislator's site without filling out a web form with your full street address. This is because legislators need to know that the people communicating with them are constituents, and the only way they can tell is if they know where you live.

Specific Takeaways

If you take away any lessons from this tactic they should be:

- Find out how this decision maker manages his or her information flow. What types of messages, and from whom, tend to generate the most attention?

- Know, with great specificity, why your communication would be relevant to the decision maker, beyond the simple fact that you think he or she should read it.

- In general, highly personalized communications from the most relevant people to the decision maker receive the most attention. These should be written using the SPIT technique discussed in Tactic 38. Then come messages from other influentials, highly relevant form communications, and unpersonalized form communications. Nigerian prince communications really aren't worth your time or the time of the audience you're trying to reach.

Tactic 27: Numbers Don't Always Matter

You've no doubt heard that numbers matter. They don't—unless you can generate amazingly high numbers. Every member of the U.S. House represents more than 750,000 people. Members of the U.S. Senate represent the population of the entire state. Fifty, a hundred—even a thousand—postcards, petitions, or blast e-mails reflect such a miniscule percentage of the legislator's overall constituency that these communications simply do not get a great deal of attention. The true value in a numbers-oriented campaign lies in helping you identify those individuals most likely to be active on your behalf. In other words, if you're able to get someone to sign a petition, you're far more likely to get that person to follow-up with a personalized e-mail or phone call. You'll need to do the work to get them to take that next step, however.

Outside of Washington, D.C., particularly in the sales or marketing world, these numbers-oriented or quantity messages often take the form of cold sales calls, postcard campaigns, or blast e-mails. Sure, these approaches can help to get your name out there, and occasionally you might get a nibble. But for most influence situations it's far more effective to target the core decision makers and personalize your message.

And don't think you're fooling anyone with that personalization software. My last name is Vance and I can't tell you how many sales e-mails I receive that start with "Dear Vance." I don't feel very special when these arrive in my e-mail inbox, certainly not special enough to respond.

Specific Takeaways

If you take away any lessons from this tactic they should be:

- Don't try to generate a numbers campaign unless you can make it tremendously impressive.
- Shortcuts in personalizing communications rarely work.

- Rather than focusing on getting many people to engage in a form-oriented effort, spend your time finding the key decision makers and crafting a personalized campaign to reach them.

- If you are going to pursue a form-oriented effort, use the feedback you receive to craft a more personalized campaign.

Tactic 28: Do *Not* Start with Your Compromise Position

You've probably heard that in Washington, D.C., budget cuts are in and spending is out. For many lobbyists, making an argument for increased funding for their cause is hard to do with a straight face. You might think that in the current economic climate it might be better to start out saying something like, "Well, we recognize that cuts need to be made so we're willing to accept this lower level of funding." But everyone in Washington knows to never, ever start with the compromise position. If you start at the compromise, you'll get even less.

Public broadcasting played this tactic perfectly during the 2011 debates on their funding levels (different aspects of which were discussed in Chapters 1, 3 and 10). Many in the community wanted to let Congress know that they understood tough budgetary times call for tough budgetary decisions. They were even willing to go to legislators and say they'd be willing to take x percentage in cuts. Champions of the effort to preserve funding led the charge against offering up this compromise at the outset. In the end, public broadcasting received level funding, something virtually unheard of for any socially oriented federal program in 2011.

Another example comes from the medical world. Physicians have been arguing for years for a permanent fix to the sustainable growth rate (SGR) formula that determines how they are reimbursed for Medicare patients. The formula was established in 1997 and has not been adjusted since then. That, combined with the fact that payments under the formula have gone down as costs have gone up, creates a profound disincentive for primary care doctors to take new Medicare patients.

The goal of the American Medical Association (AMA) and other physician groups is to permanently fix the SGR, while every year an immediate cut of between 4 and 5 percent looms. So far, Congress at the last minute every year has negated the mandated cuts and approved either a freeze or a very slight increase of about 1 percent, depending on the year.

Despite the difficulty in winning approval for changes in the original SGR formula, physicians start with that as the goal, arguing that it's hard to run a business if every year you're not sure whether you'll lose a good percentage of your revenue from the previous year. Only when it comes down to the wire do they shift from lobbying for the permanent fix to lobbying for at least the extension.

They're successful in getting the extension every year despite very real efforts to achieve fiscal responsibility and reduce waste, fraud, and abuse in the medical system. This happens for a variety of reasons, not the least of which is that they do not start with their compromise position.

Specific Takeaways

If you take away any lessons from this tactic they should be:

- Know what you want and know your compromise position. Start with the former, not the latter.
- Work with allies and champions to find out when you should go to your compromise position (this is right before the walk-away point, discussed in Tactic 30).

- Find out what you might be able to give your audience in exchange for their support on what matters most to you. Sometimes it's easy for you both to give.

Tactic 29: Trade for Votes

Unlike the previous tactic about not starting with your compromise position, for this tactic you do want to be prepared to trade something that your audience (or even your opponent) *really* wants in exchange for your support on something of importance to you. In Washington, D.C., we call this trading for votes, and it happens quite frequently between and among both members of Congress and special interest groups.

Some members of Congress, like Representative Norman ("Norm") Dicks (D-WA) excel at this. As a member of the powerful Appropriations Committee and the go-to person in the Pacific Northwest for district-based funding requests, he often put the fear of God (or the fear of Norm) into his less vaunted colleagues. Often more junior members of Congress would ask for Representative. Dicks's support on a district-based project. Norm would then ask them to vote yes on funding for something like the F/A-18 hornet military aircraft. Boeing, a major employer in Representative. Dicks's district, manufactured the airplane—one of the most expensive in the world. The vast majority of the time, Norm got his votes. Other legislators got their funding.

You may be horrified to learn that legislators trade votes for things that matter to their district. But the real lesson here is that people like deals where both sides benefit.

Specific Takeaways

If you take away any lessons from this tactic, they should be:

- Know enough about your audience to know if there's something they really want that you can give them.

- Be prepared to trade if it's compatible with your own goals.

- Remember that everyone likes win-win situations. The more you can facilitate them, the more successful you will be.

Tactic 30: Know the Walk-Away Points

If you want to learn about influence and negotiation, talk to my mother. I learned this lesson on a trip to Mexico, where she bought a beautifully embroidered denim jacket from a vendor in one of Mexico City's enormous street markets (if you're concerned about the fashion statement, it was the 1970s and denim jackets were very in).

As expected, she and the seller haggled for quite a while, reaching a point where they were within 50 cents of one another. Neither would budge. So what did my mother do? She walked away, not as a tactic, but because she knew in her heart-of-hearts that she would not pay more than her last offer. Period. End of story.

Needless to say, the vendor chased her down, gave her the jacket at her price, shook her hand, and told her she was a formidable opponent. She won because she knew when she would honestly and truly, without any doubt or reservation, walk away from the deal. Frankly, she missed a lucrative career in lobbying.

This happens a great deal in Washington, D.C., on both sides of the aisle and with both elected officials and lobbyists. As new members of Congress get elected, they are willing to walk away from more. Although some might say that this is an example of newer members being less entrenched in the system, others might argue that it takes a few years to really understand the fact that no one gets anything done without a little (or sometimes a lot) of compromise.

At the same time there are legislators with years of experience who will stick resolutely (some say stubbornly) to their positions. Representative Ron Paul (R-TX), member of the U.S. House of

Representatives and 2012 presidential candidate, votes against many pieces of legislation considered in the House of Representatives. If the vote is 434 ayes to 1 nay, much of the time that 1 is Ron Paul. His very strict libertarian beliefs prevent him from supporting most government actions. He knows when he'll walk away.

Apply this tactic to the decision makers you're approaching as well, and known when *they* will walk away. Sometimes their no is not a precursor to yes. It just means no—and usually when you hear a no from a politician that's a pretty firm no. Politicians want you to like them, which is why it's so hard for them to take definitive positions on issues. They know that someone, somewhere will be mad at them regardless of the position they take, and those people may be voters. So when they take a position that's a pretty good indication that they're at their walk-away point.

Specific Takeaways

If you take away any lessons from this tactic they should be:

- Be very clear in your own mind as to your walk-away point. Is it a certain salary level? A job title? A price point? In my experience no one is ever happy when they compromise beyond that point.

- Figure out, to the best of your ability, your audience's walk-away point. Although they may prefer your proposed solution to a problem, in any influence situation they will have other options. Don't push them past that point or they'll walk away from you.

- As Alexander Hamilton said, "Those who stand for nothing fall for anything." Never abandon your principles. When you feel like you'll need to do so, that's your walk-away point.

Tactic 31: Keep Track

Just as there are three rules of real estate (location, location, location), there are three rules of campaign plans: organize, organize, organize. All your efforts to build a structure for your cause will mean nothing without a method for keeping track of how it's going. Marcus Aurelius said, "The secret of all victory lies in the organization of the non-obvious." He was right.

I used this strategy when searching for a job after the aforementioned pink slip my boss and I got from the voters. As you'll recall, members of my political party were pretty toxic in Washington, D.C., at the time. Yet somehow I was offered two jobs on the same day just four weeks after I started looking. I achieved that goal by applying the principles in this book, one of the most important of which is keeping track.

My keeping-track process involved a spreadsheet with information on all the jobs for which I had applied including, among other things, any contact information, notes about people I knew who might be able to call on my behalf, notes about the person making the decision, where we were in the process of interviewing (where applicable), what skills they were looking for, salary range, and the timing of their decision. Within three weeks I had more than 50 entries on that spreadsheet.

Many people thought I was lucky to get a job so soon after the elections, and believe me I agree. In many ways, however, I believe I made my own luck—or at least kept track of it.

Specific Takeaways

If you take away any lessons from this tactic they should be:

- Figure out what steps you personally need to take to move you toward your goal. Tactic 3 in Chapter 2, "Set a SMART Goal" should help.

- Develop a system for keeping track of those actions. Spreadsheets, databases, and even good old-fashioned pieces of paper are appropriate options.

- If you can't make your own luck, at least keep track of it.

Tactic 32: Strategize around the Risks

You should think of your campaign plan as a gigantic chess board replete with risks to all your players. You have a number of different tools, both large and small. Your opponent has those same tools. You must see several moves ahead and know not only your options but your opponent's options. You must recognize that sometimes your initial strategy isn't working and you will need to shift your mind-set to protect your interests.

In fact, there are a few rules of chess that apply to the development of a campaign plan. First of all, don't be afraid of being checked. Chess aficionados please forgive my inadequate explanation, but this is when you need to move your king in order to prevent its capture. Sometimes you have to be checked to gain a significant advantage, such as forcing an opponent to put one of his or her pieces in danger to protect another.

Second, and this one sounds bad, but at the beginning of the game pawns can protect you. They are often dispensable. I don't mean to say that people are pawns (although sometimes we all feel as if we are). I mean that pieces of your policy agenda can be pawns. You use them at the forefront to protect other, more important pieces of your agenda. This is called starting from your strongest position and this technique is very important to legislative strategy (see Tactic 28, "Do Not Start with Your Compromise Position").

Third, the fewer significant players the other side has left, the safer you are. In the D.C. lobbying world, this usually means that if you can peel off big name supporters from the other side's perspective (and maintain your own supporters), you'll survive much longer.

Fourth, the knights are more useful than you might think. I understand that many first-time chess players are a little flummoxed by the knights. They move differently than the other pieces. But remember that the knights can move both horizontally and vertically. In many cases that gives you a huge advantage. To me, this equates to identifying both depth and breadth strategies.

Fifth, with your knight and your queen you can usually get the king cornered. If you have a knight, your queen, a bishop, and a rook left at the end of the game, you can always win, because you have pieces that can move in every direction on the board. So who are your knights, queens, bishops, and rooks in your legislative battle?

Specific Takeaways

If you take away any lessons from this tactic they should be:

- At each step of your campaign, figure out who is directly at risk.
- Know where you can move them to (1) get them out of trouble while (2) making sure you don't get another piece into trouble.
- Identify who else will be at risk if you make the move you're thinking of.
- Figure out what move you can make to limit that risk (i.e., protect someone).
- Know who it's most important to protect.
- Know ahead of time what move will gain you the most advantage.

Applying the "Develop the Campaign Plan Rule" in the Real World

Successful lobbyists pull all of these tactics together into a campaign plan. They know when to use formidable weapons, when to use simple power tools, and when to finesse their effort with something more delicate. They build influence reserves before their battle to ensure they have something to fall back on when the going gets rough. When crafting their communications strategy they avoid the Nigerian prince approach and do not focus exclusively on numbers-oriented campaigns. They are prepared to trade for votes, never start with their compromise position, and know when they (or the other side) will walk away. Finally, they keep track of their actions as well as the actions of the other side and know the risks inherent in each.

Perhaps most important, they are prepared to throw the campaign plan out as events warrant and start over again. Something like an election, a recession, or even a natural disaster can change the political field dramatically. Your influence reserve may not be enough, your compromise position might change, and the risks may start coming from other places and people. It's only when you start to believe that the structure you've built is infallible that it begins to fail. Just ask Jack Abramoff.

Chapter 8

Crafting a Winning Message

Business today consists in persuading crowds.

—T.S. Eliot

In 2009 two members of Congress from different parties, Congressman Earl Blumenauer (D-OR) and Congressman Charles Boustany (R-LA), a cardiovascular surgeon, proposed legislation to allow Medicare to cover voluntary consultations regarding lifesaving treatments. Their goal was to help patients understand all of their end-of-life options, like resuscitation requests and refusals to continue treatment.

That seems pretty reasonable, right? Well, maybe so, until someone starts calling these consultations death panels, which is exactly what Sarah Palin, former governor of Alaska, vice presidential candidate in 2008, and oft-rumored presidential candidate, did in 2009 during debate over health care reform.

That one phrase, despite widespread criticism from respected sources such as the *New York Times,* the *Economist,* the American Society of Clinical Oncology, and even commentators from the conservative Fox News program, killed (no pun intended) the idea. Based on public concerns, even though those concerns were not based on fact, legislative leaders and President Barack Obama gave up the idea of these voluntary consultations, and mention of them was removed from health care reform legislation.

I'm not suggesting that you should resort to hyperbole and hysteria to get what you want. While Palin was certainly successful in achieving one of her goals—to strike the so-called death panels from the bill—she's still nowhere near her ultimate goal of being elected to any national office. One of the reasons is that many people don't feel confident that she knows what she's talking about.

Rather, the lesson here is that the words you use can make or break your cause. That's why you'll want to craft a message that uses all the knowledge you've gained about your audience and the environment to its full advantage. The following tactics will show you how.

Tactic 33: Don't Rest on the Power of Your Position

Did you know that up until 1995 and even beyond then, cell phone companies sometimes blocked calls to 9-1-1 because the person calling did not have a roaming agreement with the carrier in the area? I was proud to be involved in ending this practice through an effort led by Congresswoman Anna Eshoo (D-CA), for whom I worked as a legislative assistant and director.

We learned about this problem when meeting with a lobbyist who told us his client's story. She tried to call 9-1-1 while being carjacked. Unfortunately, because she was traveling in an area where her cell company and the resident cell company did not have an agreement, the call was not put through. Apparently the cell phone saved her life, but only because it was pressed against the side of her face when she was shot in the head.

The cell company argued that without a roaming agreement they simply could not take responsibility for calls made in these types of situations. In addition, without the ability to locate the caller (this was before cell phones came with that technology), emergency services would have no idea where to go. And what about the potential for an overwhelming influx of emergency calls as a result of increased access? Based on their concerns about liability, technological limitations, and possible overload, cell companies and emergency service personnel formed a coalition in opposition to any efforts to require access to 9-1-1 from roaming cell phones.

Our basic argument was "Are you serious?" Nothing, we thought, would outweigh the potential to save a life. At a minimum, people should have a chance to at least *try* to reach help. After all, anyone could reach 9-1-1 through a landline phone, even if he or she had no service plan. Telephone companies were required to offer a "plug and call" service such that any phone plugged into a telephone jack could call 9-1-1. We just needed to ensure through legislative language that neither cell companies nor emergency personnel would be held liable and then everyone would agree.

Despite what we saw as our iron-clad argument, the Federal Communications Commission (FCC) almost agreed with the opposition. In 1996 the agency came very close to ruling that cell companies should not be required to cross roaming lines—until Congresswoman Eshoo made it clear that they would regret that decision. As a member of the powerful Energy and Commerce Committee with jurisdiction over the FCC, she had the ability to make things very difficult for the agency if she so chose. They decided to reevaluate the issue and eventually, after a couple years (and after I had left the office), those seeking more access to 9-1-1 won. Now, of course, anyone with a cell phone can reach 9-1-1 from wherever they have a signal (no matter whose signal it is). That fact, combined with location tracking technology, makes it far easier to reach assistance in an emergency.

Never rest on the idea that logic and compassion are on your side or believe that your position is unassailable. In our initial outreach we were pretty sure of ourselves: we assumed no one would be against giving people the ability to reach 9-1-1. We didn't think we'd really even have to argue the point.

But the issue quickly became more complicated than that, so our message evolved. Using the tragic story as a base, we talked about giving people a chance to reach help through any possible means and addressed the other side's concerns as both fixable and, in the final analysis, nowhere near as important as saving lives.

Specific Takeaways

If you take away any lessons from this tactic they should be:

- Every true cause generates some kind of opposition. Even what seems obvious can be more complex than you think.

- Those with the most logical or compassionate argument do not necessarily win.

- Know what the opposition says and shift your rhetoric to address those points. See Chapter 3 on knowing the competition for more information on how to figure that out.

Tactic 34: Connect to the Issue du Jour

With record and stubbornly high unemployment figures, the 111th and 112th Congresses (covering the time frame of January 2009 to December 2012), introduced more legislation mentioning the words *jobs* or *the economy* than at any other time in recent history.[1] In the years following the terrorist attacks of September 11, 2001, legislation addressing terrorist threats was all the rage. In fact, the world around us impacts everyone's thinking, especially decision makers. As someone seeking to influence others, you must be in tune with the big events of the day, and, as much as possible, frame your argument in that context.

For example, earlier I referred to the Repeal of the Job Killing Health Care Reform Act. This title makes it pretty clear how the

---

[1]www.congress.gov.

authors view health care reform (and what they want to do about it). But notice they did not call it the Repeal of the Access-to-Care Killing Health Care Reform Act, or the Repeal of the Health Care Reform Act that Will Endanger Our Citizens Act, or even the Repeal of the Health Care Reform Bill That's Mean to Children and Seniors Act. The focus was on jobs, because that's the topic du jour.

We also see this with education reform. Every few years the federal programs associated with education services must go through a renewal process. Legislators hope to review what has worked, what hasn't, and to update funding levels accordingly. This renewal process (known as reauthorization) also forwards the agendas of the political parties associated with government leaders.

When it came time to reauthorize the Elementary and Secondary Education Act (which authorizes specific types and levels of federal funding for K-12 schools and services), the issue du jour was family values. Everyone talked pretty much nonstop about helping families and America's children. President George W. Bush sought to take advantage of this atmosphere by referring to his package of renewal proposals as the No Child Left Behind Act. No one wants to leave children behind ever, but this way of titling the legislation was particularly relevant at the time.

For your own influence situation, figure out the issue du jour and find the best way to connect your cause to that issue. Remember that the issue du jour may change over time, and shift your message accordingly.

Specific Takeaways

If you take away any lessons from this tactic they should be:

- Review newspapers, magazines, television and radio news programs, Internet outlets, and the like to figure out the issue du jour being discussed by everyone in the country (or the world, for that matter).

- Capture your audience's attention by connecting your cause to that issue.

Tactic 35: Do *Not* Be Insulting—Whether on Purpose, in Secret or by Accident

Sometimes people came to our congressional office with some variation of this kind of rudeness: "I know the congressman never agrees with me and that he's pretty ignorant. I'm sure he takes money from the other side and that's the only reason why he votes the way he does. But, I'm supposed to come talk to you, so do you think the congressman would sponsor this legislation I know he hates?"

This is not very influential. Yet you would be surprised at the number of people who start their initial plea for their case with incredibly insulting statements. Or consider this approach: "As a tax-payer, I pay your salary, you bloated bureaucrat, so you have to do what I say." In this case I would hand a dime to the person I was meeting with and call it even. Ten cents was the result of my salary divided by the number of people we represented.

I remember a very unpleasant meeting with a lobbyist who came in to our congressional office convinced that we were holding out on vital information about the consideration of a certain policy issue. She was sure it was going to be considered soon, and we had no idea what she was talking about. After the meeting I went to the rest-room down the hall, where I overheard her talking to her colleague using words like *deceitful* and *dishonest*. They were, of course, talking about my boss. I never let them know I overheard. I also never met with that lobbyist again.

Finally, try not to even unintentionally insult people. Sometimes we forget to self-edit before we let words come out of our mouths. I, for example, once spoke to a group interested in racial diversity, which included a number of Native Americans. While giving my presentation I used some very insensitive language involving the phrase "off the reservation." Super, super offensive. I'm embarrassed to even type it here.

I also catch myself doing this with visually impaired advocates. You'd be surprised at the number of times you say the word *see* in a presentation. Perhaps the most embarrassing situation was in a presentation to the American Ambulance Association. Members of the organization included emergency medical technicians, equipment manufacturers, and the like. I referred to them as "ambulance drivers," a perfectly innocent mistake. But the response I got was, well, not flattering. I really put my foot in my mouth.

Now I solve this problem (or at least mitigate it) by asking my client if there are words or phrases that are big no-no's with the group. This tactic benefited me greatly when speaking recently with the Council of State Restaurant Associations shortly after sexual misconduct allegations were made (and subsequently confirmed) against former presidential candidate (and previous president of the National Restaurant Association) Herman Cain. I confirmed with them before my presentation that I should avoid all discussion of this issue—even in jest. The directors of the organization appreciated my foresight—and discretion.

Specific Takeaways

If you take away any lessons from this tactic they should be:

- Avoid overt insults, unless you never plan to speak to that decision maker again.
- Don't badmouth your audience, even in private. It will often get back to them.

- Remember to think ahead of time about what your audience may find insulting. Sometimes you might even ask just to be sure.

- Feel free to think whatever you want. Just don't say it.

Tactic 36: Find the Common Ground

In politics, almost every outcome comes through compromise regardless of whether that result makes everyone equally happy or equally miserable. Sure, it may be possible to pass a resolution to name a post office in honor of Elvis or proclaiming National Pickle Week without trading for votes or compromising on the language, although a lengthy discussion could ensue on, for example, how one defines *pickle*. Is it just gherkins? Sweet pickles? What about pickle slices versus spears?

The best way to promote compromise is to remember that, for the most part, everyone believes they have a good reason for their particular position. You may not think it's a good reason. You may believe that they are horribly misguided. But *they* see it as a good reason and will likely be as tenacious as you. In that case, sometimes you must be the grown-up and seek the common ground.

This let's all be grown-ups approach works even in Washington, D.C. One of the congressional offices I worked for used this technique in seeking to protect what we saw as an important program to finance Internet access and hardware for schools and libraries. The program was called the E-rate, although those who didn't like it called it the Gore tax after then Vice President, Al Gore (see the discussion at the start of this chapter regarding how language can impact an issue). Several members of Congress opposed the program for a variety of reasons. For example, they didn't think the federal government should spend money on it, or they believed it interfered with free enterprise. Yet we needed these members to either vote no on ending the program or at least let leadership know they didn't want it to come up (see the section in Tactic 18 on maintaining rank-and-file neutrality). If we were to succeed.

The members of Congress with whom we found the most common ground were those who opposed the program on the grounds that it would increase access to child pornography. No one really supported an outcome of more pornography on the Internet. So we worked with the other side to add in language requiring filtering technology. On our side we weren't thrilled about the potential additional administrative burden. On their side they weren't thrilled about the continuation of the program. But we were all able to play nicely together—at least on that issue.

In some influence situations, you will get the decision maker to say "yes" only with the agreement of another party and, unfortunately sometimes that other party may disagree with you. Remember that they probably feel as strongly about their perspective on your cause as you do about yours. For example, it's likely that a rival company really feels that their product or service out-performs yours. In many cases you'll probably want to simply "win out" using many of the other tactics in this book. But in some situations there may be opportunities to reach out and find the common ground.

Specific Takeaways

If you take away any lessons from this tactic they should be:

- Sometimes you'll need someone else's help or at least their nonopposition to get your primary decision maker to say yes.

- That someone may disagree with your perspective and they'll feel as strongly about their side as you do about yours.

- Even though they may clearly be wrong, start assessing from the beginning whether there's any common ground. You may need to reach it in order to move forward.

Tactic 37: Remember the Puppies and Children Rule

Due to my somewhat irrational love of animals (my dog has a Facebook page), the members of Congress for whom I worked often assigned me animal welfare issues. Having someone with a soft spot for puppies and kitties always helped when meeting with special interest groups like the Humane Society of the United States or the American Society for the Prevention of Cruelty to Animals. As such, I was the one who received most of the mail about any animal-related legislation.

One memorable issue revolved around a proposed bill called the Pet Protection Act. Supporters argued that it would make it a federal crime to steal someone's pet and sell it to a research facility or for other nefarious purposes, such as dog-fighting. Some called the legislation unnecessary, because stealing someone's pet isn't allowed in any jurisdiction. However, it's not a federal crime, which carries additional penalties and would hopefully act as a stronger deterrent. (It should be noted that opponents to the legislation believed pet stealing was not as rampant as some would suggest and that local jurisdictions had the authority to manage any cases.)

We had received about a hundred postcards from constituents asking my boss to lend his support to the bill. As you might imagine, we weren't particularly opposed to the idea. But the issue never really rose to the top of our priority list—until we received a personal letter from a woman in our district. Her pet had been stolen and, in fact, a small pet-thieving ring had taken other animals in the area. The police never recovered her two-month-old Labrador retriever puppy. She even sent a picture. But then the kicker came—she said she had kids and asked, "How am I supposed to tell my kids what happened to the puppy?"

By the end of the letter I was practically in tears, crying "I don't know! This is terrible! Someone needs to do something about it!"

That someone was us and the letter convinced my boss to cosponsor the legislation. Though, of course, the one member of Congress I worked for did not single-handedly enact the ban, he did play an important role in moving the issue forward. Years later (yes, it took years), President George W. Bush signed the Animal Fighting Prohibition Enforcement Act, which included provisions to address the parts of this problem specifically related to stealing dogs for dog-fighting purposes.

This story highlights the power of two tactics: (1) personalized communications work significantly better than form letters [see Tactics 26 and 27] and (2), where possible invoke what we call the puppies and children argument. Sure, your particular cause may not relate specifically back to puppies and children as obviously as this one. That said, do what you can to cultivate any arguments that may tug at heartstrings. They are more powerful than you can imagine.

And if the puppies and children rule doesn't work, consider adopting a catch phrase. Representative Jim Traficant (D-OH) gave speeches on the floor of the House of Representatives almost every day. He ended every single speech with the phrase "Beam me up, Mr. Speaker," paraphrasing what members of the crew of the Starship Enterprise said when wanting to be teleported back to the ship. His words suggested that the House of Representatives has a bit of a science fiction quality to its proceedings. He was also known for trying to attach buy-American provisions to every relevant bill moving through the Congress (and to many nonrelevant bills as well).

Of course, Representative Traficant was convicted of 10 felony counts, including bribery and racketeering and spent seven years in federal prison, so perhaps he isn't the best example of ethical influence. But even before all that, we sure remembered him—and his message. His green felt sports jackets probably helped, but please don't resort to such extreme measures.

Crafting a Winning Message

Specific Takeaways

If you take away any lessons from this tactic they should be:

- Consider whether there's a *believable* heartstrings argument you can make for your cause.

- Move your argument beyond your self-interest to focus on how others might benefit.

- Where possible, consider developing a memorable catch phrase. "Beam me up, Mr. Speaker" is already taken, but you may be able to find another.

Tactic 38: Use the SPIT Formula

I've lost count of the number of acronyms in this book, but there are lots of them. Clearly, everyone in Washington, D.C., loves acronyms, so naturally I developed one for effective message development. It's SPIT, which stands for specific, personal, informative, and timely, and it incorporates many of the tactics already discussed into one big happy formula for success.

Specific in Terms of What You Want

As noted in Chapter 2, it is essential that you know what you want and be able and willing to ask for it. The question "What can I do for you?" must not be met with blank stares. It's not a rhetorical question: decision makers really want to know how they can help.

Specific in Terms of What the Audience Wants

In addition to clarity about what you want, look for ways to connect your ask to what the audience wants. Your research into the perspectives and interests of your audience will assist you. It's not enough to say, "I know this will really help you." You'll want to say, "I saw that you want to do *x*. This will really help you do that because . . ." For example, "I saw in your company's annual report that you want to increase your profits by 10 percent this year. This product will save you *x* number of hours per week in staff time, leaving significantly more time for those business development activities necessary to help you achieve your goal."

Personal

You attract people to your cause through a compelling story, something politicians do all the time. If you ever watch the annual State of the Union address, you'll notice that presidents often highlight the activities of ordinary people who have done extraordinary things, such as Captain Chesley B. "Sully" Sullenberger who saved 155 people when he "landed" U.S. Airways flight 1549 in the Hudson River in January 2009.

Ronald Reagan was the first president to employ this tactic, inviting Lenny Skutniks, a retired Congressional Budget Office employee, to join Mrs. Reagan in the gallery during his 1982 State of the Union address. According to the president, Mr. Skutniks embodied the "spirit of American heroism," for diving into the freezing Potomac River to rescue a stranded passenger after the 1982 crash of Air Florida flight 90 near National Airport in the D.C. metro area. That speech was lauded as one of the best ever from Reagan, who was known for giving great speeches.

In fact, the ploy was so successful that every president since has, at one time or another, presented a special guest—and his or her story—as part of their State of the Union address. The people mentioned in these speeches are referred to as "Lenny Skutniks."

This approach works because people naturally pay attention to stories. It's interesting and heartening to hear about one person's courage to save a stranger at the risk of his or her own life. We want to know more, right? Who was the person who was rescued? Did he or she live? What happened to Lenny after that? If this were a Hollywood movie, we'd probably also hope that Lenny and the rescued passenger fell in love and got married (didn't happen).

Stories also make the cause tangible. We know through a story that the thing we're talking about has had, or will have, an impact on an actual human being. It's not theoretical; it's real. Think how less effective it would have been for President Reagan to say "Americans are heroic—I know of a guy who once saved a lady from a plane crash."

As you're crafting your influence message, think about that story—what can you say about yourself, someone you care about or, if possible, someone the decision maker cares about, to make your cause real? What can you say that will initially capture the decision maker's attention—and make him or her want to learn more?

Informative

Lobbyists in the medical community juxtapose the personal story and the informative argument very well. When lobbying on the issue of Medicare reimbursement (which, as noted in Tactic 28, is threatened with major cuts every year), doctors often tell the story about a specific patient who needs Medicare to survive and then will give statistics on the impacts in each state. The combination of logic and heartstrings has worked so far to prevent the cuts.

A legislator or, really, any decision maker will also want to know what the opposition thinks about your cause. In providing that information yourself, you demonstrate you have nothing to fear from the competition. It also gives you a chance to explain why they are horribly misguided. Although this may seem self-defeating, remember that the decision maker you're working with will almost certainly hear from the other side anyway. In preempting that by providing all sides of the story, you make your argument both more informative and trustworthy.

Timely

Often, people call congressional offices when they're upset about how the member of Congress voted. They rant, they rave—sometimes they even make the staff person cry. I used to point out that the best time to have received this information would have been before the vote, not after. They invariably responded that they *would* have called, but they knew we would never have paid attention. "Yep," I thought, "That's a sure way not to be heard—don't speak up."

Clearly, contacting a decision maker after a decision has been made rarely works, and it's equally ineffective to contact a decision maker too early. Circumstances may change around your initial contact and the time of the decision. Unless they're a champion or strong supporter (see Tactic 18), most decision makers will not want to be on the record in support or opposition to something that might not even happen. Your job is to build a relationship with the decision maker over time so that when the issue does come up, your specific ask is a no-brainer.

In addition, remember that your audience probably is nowhere near as focused on your cause as you are. It's your cause, after all, not theirs. So although you want to spend time building a relationship, nagging them about a specific decision that's not even on the table yet rarely makes sense.

To achieve all this, consider using the following formula.

Knowing of your interest in x (specific to the audience), I thought you'd be interested in y (specific in terms of what you want).

This is important to me because (personal story). In addition, I believe this would benefit you because (informative facts). I understand you'll be making a decision by (timely). Are you willing/able to (your specific ask)?

Specific Takeaways

If you take away any lessons from this tactic they should be:

- A specific, personal, informative, and timely (SPIT) message helps pull together all the information you've gathered about your audience and the issue into one comprehensive pitch.
- Be specific in terms of what you want (the ask) as well as why the decision maker you're targeting would be interested.
- To the extent you can, tell an honest personal story.
- Bring relevant facts, figures, and statistics to the table, particularly those related to the personal story.
- Make your pitch before (but not too far before) the decision time frame.

Applying the Crafting the Message Rule in the Real World

Marshall McLuhan, a Canadian scholar and literary critic, famously said, "The medium is the message." I always interpreted this to mean that the tool we use to deliver our message has more to do with how persuasive we are than what we actually say.

Frankly, I've never agreed with that, particularly as it relates to Capitol Hill. The message is the message, plain and simple. It really won't matter how you deliver a message if the language isn't right, but the right language can advance your cause by light years. Personal, thoughtful, relevant communications that are not insulting will, after a time, rise to the top. Sure, some delivery techniques (such as meetings—see Chapter 9 for more on delivery strategies) may advance the profile of an issue more quickly, but the basic language and content of the message should remain the same.

To craft that message, start with recognizing that you should never rest on what you may see as an unassailable argument. In most influence situations, someone somewhere will oppose you. To be most persuasive, develop the core of your message—basically what you want and why it's important to you. To delve further, focus on identifying different angles based on the issue du jour or an effort to find common ground.

Oh, and if you can work puppies, kittens, or children into your message, you really should.

Chapter 9

Delivering the Message

Chapter 9

Delivering the Message

No matter how carefully you plan your goals they will never be more than pipe dreams unless you pursue them with gusto.

—W. Clement Stone

Despite all that talk in Chapter 8 about the supremacy of message content over the delivery medium, figuring out how the best way get your message out there is nonetheless an important issue. Your choices will depend on what your audience wants, who is delivering the message, timing, the outlets available, and what's happening in the world at large. The following tactics will help you determine which tools you should use as well as how to use them most effectively to deliver your message.

Tactic 39: Pick the Delivery Method That Works for Your Audience, Not You

I'm amazed by people who claim that a certain method of communication—an in-person meeting or a phone call, for example—is always better than anything else. Of course, I'm one of the worst offenders, frequently espousing e-mail as the best way to communicate. For me, I find I can better organize my thoughts and respond when I'm able to do so (often at midnight). Phone call interruptions during the day tend to really irritate me. So if I'm your customer or you want to sell me something, you better be e-mailing.

On the other hand, if you're my client or a prospective client, I'll do my best to use your preferred delivery method (unless you like phone calls and I won't do that to you at midnight). The easiest way to find out how your audience wants to hear your message is to ask. Once you've figured that out, use the following tips for using that delivery method to your advantage.

Meetings

If you're going to request a meeting, you must be able to answer the question, "Why would this person want to meet with me?" You know why you want to meet with them. But their time is just as valuable as yours—and they need to think the meeting is worthwhile as well.

In my very first couple weeks as a staff person on Capitol Hill, hordes of lobbyists asked to meet with me. They wanted to put a face with a name, and learn a little bit about me. I wanted to get work done. One of the people in my office described these as "meetlings," or little meetings, suggesting, in a very cynical way, that these interactions were valuable for the lobbyist requesting the meeting mainly because he or she could charge the client for an hour of time (which included travel to and from the meeting). With Washington, D.C., prices at hundreds of dollars an hour, those meetlings were certainly profitable, but not always for me.

When the smart, effective lobbyists called to request a meeting, they explained briefly over the phone how they connected to our constituents, what issues they were most interested in, and how to reach them if I had questions. They also, and I cannot stress this enough, asked me if a meeting would be helpful to me. If they had made a strong enough case for how their cause connected to my boss's job (and hence mine), I met with them.

As one congressional staff person I know put it: "As a lobbyist you get one 'Hey, how are you doing?' meeting per year. After that, you better want to meet about something." This person belongs to the opposite political party to my own, by the way, so this feeling is completely bipartisan. That said, I know plenty of congressional staff who like meetings. The best lobbyists know who those staff are, and communicate with them accordingly.

Telephone

Lobbyists recognize that decision makers probably aren't sitting around waiting for the phone to ring. To increase effectiveness and decrease the interruption factor, they follow a few simple rules. First, and most important, they ask, "Do you prefer phone calls or e-mail?" If the decision maker likes e-mail, they start with that.

Second, if the lobbyist thinks it will take more than 10 or 15 minutes to discuss the issue, they'll make a phone appointment. When they do catch someone on the phone, even if it's a phone appointment, they ask, "Is this still a good time to talk?" Schedules change quickly on Capitol Hill. Floor votes, committee hearings, and caucus meetings can all come up at the last minute.

In addition, lobbyists use voice mail effectively, leaving their name and phone number (and/or e-mail) early in the message, a sentence telling the decision maker who they are (even if it's a reminder), and a sentence on the purpose of their call. Unless you're close to the decision maker, an informal message is neither appropriate nor effective. The decision maker may not even remember who you are! If you're going to leave a voice mail, consider using something along the lines of the following formula:

Hello, this is Stephanie Vance from Advocacy Associates. My number is (_____) or you can reach me on e-mail at (_____). The best times to reach me are (_____). We met a couple weeks ago to discuss (_____). I'm calling to see if you've made a decision or if I can answer any questions you may have.

There's no guarantee using that approach will generate a return phone call, but it's probably more likely to do so than something more informal.

Fax

Over the course of several years on Capitol Hill, I cannot remember a morning where I was not confronted with 20 to, sometimes, 500 faxes on our fax machine. Several members of Congress had to change their fax number every few months to prevent a complete shutdown of the line. That said, some people work better with paper so they still prefer faxes. In general, these are the same people who print out their e-mail. It's not my thing, but if it's your audience's thing, do it.

E-Mail

According to the Congressional Management Foundation (CMF), the Capitol Hill e-mail servers processed more than 200 million e-mails in 2004. In 2011 a report from CMF found that House and Senate offices had experienced an increase of between 200 and 1,000 percent in the number of communications, particularly in 2009-2010 with all the fun over health care reform. Even using the lowest numbers, that's upward of 1 billion e-mails coming in to Capitol Hill each year. And you thought you got a lot of e-mails.

Despite these huge numbers, e-mail can be a very effective method for getting your message across, but only if you remember that all the basic rules for effective messages apply to e-mails as well. On Capitol Hill that translates to being directed, relevant, specific, personalized, and, most important, brief.

Special interests and lobbyists direct their e-mails by addressing them to the specific congressional staff person they're trying to reach. Frankly, an e-mail to an info@rep-so-and-so.gov box saying, "Please pass this along to the relevant staff person," will get lost. As noted in Tactic 26, these days it's impossible to send an e-mail to a general congressional inbox. You must fill out a web form to fill in your complete address in order to demonstrate you are a constituent. Lobbyists send e-mails directly to staff people with whom they have a relationship and then make those e-mails relevant by connecting the message back to that legislator's specific interests or district. They're specific about what they want and they do all of this in one screen. As a congressional staff person once told one of the special interest groups I was working with, "Your job is to trick the computer. You need to get past all our automated methods for dealing with e-mail and get to me, a human being." Lobbyists and special interests excel at this.

Social Media

There's a lot of talk these days about using social media approaches to deliver a message to Capitol Hill. However, most lobbyists and special interests find it to be more useful for gauging advocate interests, engaging others in the debate, and learning about legislators. In other words, although legislators like to use social media to share their views, its use as a way to deliver a persuasive message from a citizen to a legislator is not yet proven.

This is because, in part, the legislator cannot tell if the person communicating with him or her is a constituent. And though we would all like to imagine that democracy should be about everyone sharing his or her views with everyone, representative democracy works a little differently. The most persuasive messages come from a constituent and you can't tell whether people are constituents if you don't know their physical location.

That said, if you can demonstrate relevancy to the decision maker, social media can be a good way to get his or her attention. In addition, these strategies can be very useful tools for researching your audience. Following them on Facebook, YouTube, and Twitter; seeing what groups they're in; and checking out your mutual friends will tell you a great deal about what interests them. You can also use these sources, and particularly a site like LinkedIn, to figure out who already knows the person you're trying to influence. Who knows? You may be one or two degrees separated from someone who already has a connection—and that person may be willing to become a champion or supporter.

Postal Mail

It's hard to say what works when sending postal mail to Capitol Hill because all pieces of paper being sent to the House and Senate office buildings must be irradiated first. This process takes some time and the letters come out brown, crunchy, and smelling bad. Not so influential. The main lesson that translates to the real world is similar to that of e-mail: remember that any mass communication will likely be thrown away. Personalization is the rule here as well.

Be Merciful

Whatever method you pick, remember that while you are focusing on your goal with a laserlike focus, your audience is probably dealing with a whole host of other issues. You want to find a balance between keeping on their radar screen versus irritating them to the point of alienation.

Bradford Fitch, president and chief executive officer of the Congressional Management Foundation, tells the story of representatives from a powerful interest group who met with a staff person for a legislator on a key committee. The group was interested in getting the lawmaker to cosponsor a particular bill they favored. When they didn't get a response soon enough (the lawmaker had a hearing scheduled on the legislation), they sent everyone in their large organization the chief of staff's direct line. That action shut down the phone lines for the office. This was not well-received by the congressional office—an office that otherwise might have been inclined to work with them. Some even suggested that the group's action constituted a denial of service attack and should be subject to criminal charges.

Careful readers may note that the tactic of flooding the lines proved effective in an earlier example (the American Library Association and its efforts to defeat a rule regarding the toxic substance lead in books, discussed in the Introduction). The difference here is that librarians were asked to call the public feedback line regarding a very specific, immediate, and hugely damaging proposal. This other group, on the other hand, handed out a private phone number and asked its members to call because they thought something that would benefit them should move faster. Effective lobbyists always match their tactic to their situation.

Before you start delivering your message, check out Tactic 43 on persistence versus stalking. You do not want to cross that line.

Specific Takeaways

If you take away any lessons from this tactic they should be:

- Recognize that not everyone communicates the same way you do.
- Ask your audience which method of communication they prefer and then use that one.
- For meetings, be sure the decision maker knows why they would want to meet with you. Why are you relevant to that person?

- For phone calls, be respectful of their time and ask for a phone meeting if appropriate.

- For e-mail, remember that fewer personalized communications work far better than blast e-mail campaigns.

- For social media, consider the idea that the true value may be not in bombarding the decision maker with messages but in conducting research.

- For postal mail, apply the same rules as e-mail—and know whether irradiation is a possibility.

- Finally, be merciful. Your goal should not be to shut down the communication method you're using. Your goal should be to have the message delivered.

Tactic 40: Have the Proper Materials

How do you define *proper materials?* A former chief of staff for a Republican member of Congress described to me the perfect example of improper materials in the context of Washington, D.C. He met with a group that presented him with a very large binder, beautifully engraved with the elected official's name. The organization's not unreasonable plan was to periodically send talking points, articles, and other information about their cause to the office and provided the binder as a storage mechanism.

What they did not understand is that congressional staffers have very limited space for storing materials. The staffer in question thanked them and, when they left, took the most useful materials out of the binder (the executive summary and their contact information) and threw the binder in the Dumpster outside.

The group came back to the office later in the day and, for reasons I never entirely understood, apparently went Dumpster diving. They found the binder, which, as aforementioned, was very usefully printed with the legislator's name. Outraged, they demanded an explanation. Somewhat chagrined, the chief of staff took them back to his desk, showed them the tiny cubicle in which he worked, and explained the problem. To their credit, the group understood and changed their tactics when it came to providing materials.

Most busy decision makers do not have time for 17-page dissertations on why they should agree with you. In fact, if your perspective is right, it should not take 17 pages—or even 5 pages—to make your point. After a meeting on Capitol Hill, lobbyists leave behind what's called a one-pager, outlining the issues discussed and the organization's policy or funding ask. They supply additional information only after they've been asked for it.

Effective lobbyists also provide materials that demonstrate the direct impact of a certain position on that legislator's best interests. Another chief of staff I know makes note of a group that left behind a map of the representative's congressional district that included statistics on how many of those who voted in the recent election were members of their organization. It was a large group and a sizable number of people. Imagine the power of showing that hundreds or perhaps thousands of voters in the legislator's district support a particular policy position.

Although there's no hard and fast rule about what constitutes proper materials, a good rule of thumb is to simply give whatever the decision maker asks for. If the person you're trying to influence asks for no more than 5 pages of a writing sample, 20 pages will not impress them. It will irritate them. Rather than demonstrating that you can write a long piece (even if it's interesting), you demonstrate that you cannot follow directions. In almost every influence situation this is not desired.

Sure, in some cases, such as applying for that perfect job, you may be asked for an extensive listing of your accomplishments and experience. You should always give the decision maker the choice. And if his

165

Delivering the Message

or her preference isn't clear, ask. For more on this, see Tactic 17, "Know What They Need From You, Not What You Want to Give Them."

Specific Takeaways

If you take away any lessons from this tactic they should be:

- More is rarely better than less when it comes to materials. Exactly the right amount of information trumps everything else.

- Take steps to know what you've been asked for. Do not provide what you think the decision maker should have. Provide what *they* think they need and let them ask for more.

- Make the materials as relevant to the decision maker as possible. Your research into what wakes them up in the morning and keeps them up at night (Tactic 16) will help.

- If you have no idea what the decision maker wants, ask.

Tactic 41: Turn Lemons into Lemonade

In October 2011, Terry Thompson, owner of the Muskingum County Animal Farm in Zanesville, Ohio, released his 56 exotic animals into the surrounding populated area and committed suicide. Law enforcement officers shot and killed 49 of the animals at close range, one monkey was believed to have been eaten by some of the released predators, and six were brought to the Columbus Zoo. Animal activists pointed out that Ohio has some of the weakest regulations in the United States on keeping exotic animals.

Three days after the tragedy, The Humane Society of the United States sent an action alert asking that advocates contact policymakers to support proposed legislation banning the import of exotic animals. Days after the event, Ohio Governor John Kasich signed an executive order to shut down animal auctions and give more power to animal-protection officers. New laws are being drafted that would ban the sale of these animals to anyone who is not a professional handler.

Whether you agree with that policy or not, the Humane Society clearly understood how to turn lemons into lemonade when it came to these events. Although the situation was tragic, they used it as an opportunity to move forward on an issue that had stagnated.

Specific Takeaways

If you take away any lessons from this tactic they should be:

- Look at negative events as potential opportunities to demonstrate the problem you're trying to solve.

- Take immediate and specific action to tie that event to your cause.

Tactic 42: No Astroturf

Not even those who manufacture or sell artificial grass refer to it as Astroturf any more. I know this because the Synthetic Turf Council is a client of ours. The word *Astroturf* clearly has negative connotations, both in Washington, D.C., and in the marketplace.

Just how bad is it? In 2009 a grassroots consulting firm named Bonner and Associates was hired to strengthen grassroots opposition to the American Clean Energy and Security Act. The goal was to convince a key player, Representative Tom Perriello (D-VA), to vote against the legislation. Their strategies were similar to those outlined here: they learned about Representative. Perriello's background and interests and they asked constituent groups associated with those interests to send a letter to the representative's office opposing the bill.

Unfortunately, one of their employees forged a letter from the local chapter of the National Association for the Advancement of

Colored People that was signed by someone who did not exist. The content was forged, the letterhead was forged and, of course, the signature was forged (although the question remains, is it forgery if you're signing for a nonexistent person?).

Clearly what the Bonner and Associates staff person did is illegal, but many people see any effort to get information out about an issue and to help local groups respond as the communication equivalent of "Astroturf" inauthentic at best and deceitful at worst. In D.C., it's interpreted as helping to generate messages based not on the sender's true perspective on an issue, but on something more artificial.

The best description of legal but ineffective Astroturf strategies are those in which an organization or a business asks people to get involved by writing a letter or sending an e-mail, with a "don't worry about what the message is just sign it" attitude. Although many advocates may choose not to communicate a personal message instead of the message created by the organization, to avoid an appearance of Astroturf the sponsoring organization should at least be sure the person sending it knows what it says and has the opportunity to personalize it should they choose to.

Specific Takeaways

If you take away any lessons from this tactic they should be:

- Don't twist other people's arms to get engaged in your cause. Their messages will not be influential if they aren't honest.
- Get others involved in your effort in ways that allow them to express their true support for your cause.
- Don't forge things.

Applying the Delivering the Message Rule in the Real World: Lather, Rinse, Repeat

As you evaluate the effectiveness of your delivery methods, you'll want to use the lather, rinse, repeat strategy. First, lather up with what you consider, based on your research, to be the most effective surrogates and give them the most appropriate messages, facts and figures, and delivery strategies. Be prepared to deliver these messages yourself as well.

Then, as you're implementing your campaign, review your lather up strategy in the context of the benchmarks you've created. Rinse through anything that's not working and revise your strategy accordingly. Repeat the process until you've succeeded. Don't worry—you'll get there, particularly if you're effective in playing the end game, which we discuss next.

Chapter 10

The End Game

Ninety-nine percent of success in life is showing up.

—Woody Allen

The other 1 percent is following up.

—The Advocacy Guru's Own Addition

Although many special interests show up, the vast majority never follow-up, and those that do, impress those they are trying to influence with their ongoing commitment to their issue. Even with an incredibly brilliant, relevant, personalized message delivered by the most influential surrogates you can find, it's rare to get what you want the first time you ask. How you play the end game will determine how far you go and, ultimately, whether you succeed or fail.

Tactic 43: Know the Difference between Persistence and Stalking

In 1973 Emily Sheketoff, now executive director of the Washington office of the American Library Association (ALA), served as a staff person to Senator Lowell Weicker, a member of the Watergate committee. It was one of her first jobs in Washington, D.C. As you no doubt recall, the Watergate committee convened to investigate what become known as the Watergate scandal. Officials of the Nixon administration were found guilty of many nefarious activities, such

173

as wiretapping, breaking and entering—you know, pretty standard D.C. stuff.

Emily became very popular as a result of this association. Reporters and other congressional staff lurked outside the secret, windowless committee room where she worked to see what information they could extract from her or others who witnessed any of the proceedings.

On one memorable occasion, Lesley Stahl, a high-profile reporter for CBS (and incidentally the reporter who interviewed Jack Abramoff for the *60 Minutes* segment on his own notorious lobbying activities), pounced on Emily right after Nixon administration official Alexander Butterfield had revealed in a private meeting that wiretapping was a pretty common practice in the Nixon administration. The hearing had been held on a Friday and it was imperative that the information not be leaked to the media over the weekend. Investigators did not want to give anyone an opportunity to remove evidence.

Emily told Lesley, politely but firmly, that she could not tell her anything. Nevertheless, like any good media person Lesley persisted. She followed her quarry into the ladies restroom and continued to press her while Emily was, as we say, using the facilities. Emily stayed in the stall for 20 minutes, just waiting for an opportunity to escape. Lesley never got a word out of her.

Following up occasionally with a phone call or e-mail is persistence. Following your quarry into the bathroom is stalking. The decision maker you're pursuing will probably give off signals when you've crossed the line. You can usually tell when they begin ignoring your every effort at communication.

If they aren't returning your e-mails, a follow-up phone call may be in order. If they don't return your e-mails *or* your phone calls, that's a pretty good sign that additional communications will not be welcomed and you should back off. If you're e-mailing them, calling them, texting them, and sending messages through Facebook and Twitter without any responses, you've gone too far.

Keeping track of ongoing conversations can also help your goal of persisting without being irritating. For example, when our firm works to set up a meeting between a constituent and a congressional office, we make very careful notes about what the scheduler tells us in terms of their time frame for getting back to us. If they say, "We won't make a decision on that until such-and-such a date," there's no point in reaching out to them before that date. That additional outreach serves only to waste our time and irritate them.

Remember too that you can improve your chances of gaining their attention by choosing a mode of communication they prefer (see Tactic 39). And if building rapport is proving particularly difficult, try to communicate through someone your decision maker already talks to (see Chapter 6, "Find Your Surrogates—The 'Influentials'"). That person is far more likely to capture his or her attention than you are.

Specific Takeaways

If you take away any lessons from this tactic they should be:

- There's a difference between being persistent and being a pest.

- Learn to recognize the signals that may indicate you have crossed a line. Usually, if your audience is ignoring two methods of communication (e-mail and phone, for example), they really aren't interested in talking to you.

- Find the best option for sending a message to the decision maker without creeping them out or violating their specific instructions. Doing some research to find a direct e-mail address is okay. Stalking the decision maker and sending a letter to his or her home is not—neither is making a phone call when an ad says, "No phone calls please."

- Keep track of the time frame in which they said they'd make a decision and schedule your follow-up accordingly.

- You can improve your chances of gaining their attention by using the mode of communication they prefer or by finding a surrogate to help.

- Don't follow them into the bathroom.

Tactic 44: Control the Uncontrollable

On September 11, 2001, the U.S. House was scheduled to consider the Consequences for Juvenile Offenders Act, the Small Business Liability Relief and Brownfields Revitalization Act, and to meet with the prime minister of Australia. The Senate planned to continue debate on appropriations for the Commerce Department. Then, at 8:46 A.M. a plane crashed into the World Trade Center, to be followed by a plane crashing into the Pentagon, and a plane, bound for the White House or Capitol, crashing into a cornfield in Pennsylvania. For the next month, at least, almost every congressional hearing and debate related to additional funding for the war on terror. Two weeks later, the U.S. military began a war on Iraq. Needless to say, every other issue fell by the wayside.

Sometimes, external events overtake your effort to promote your cause and there's really nothing you can do about it. This happens often in Washington, D.C., where lobbyists and special interests make the mistake of trying to figure out how they can force Congress to stop talking about whatever external issue is going on and start talking about their cause.

Frankly, it's not possible. There's no amount of money or political favors or good old-fashioned logical arguments you can throw at a legislator to make him or her stop talking about the issue du jour. Rather than making this completely futile effort, an effective lobbyist figures out how his or her cause connects to the issue du jour—and then talks about that (Tactic 34 "Connect to the Issue du Jour" shows you how.)

For example, in September 2005 after Hurricane Katrina, the issues of disaster recovery and emergency preparedness reigned in Washington, D.C. Anyone who was anyone introduced legislation about this or that natural or unnatural calamity. In fact, 355 bills mentioning hurricanes were introduced in the four months following the event. That's compared to 28 in the previous two-year congressional term.

At the same time, most of the major appropriations bills that fund the workings of the government had not yet been finalized for the fiscal year starting October 1. Many special interests, particularly those who had not been directly impacted by Katrina, were in a quandary. How should they make their case with legislators in light of the current tragedy gripping the nation?

The smart lobbyists took stock of their issue and reframed their message in a way consistent with the current conversation. Libraries, for example, focused on the physical resources lost in the flood, making the point that funding for electronic databases would limit the damage in the future. The U.S. Chamber of Commerce focused its message on both the job loss associated with the hurricane as well as opportunities to bring New Orleans back through economic development funds. Public television and radio stations let legislators know how dollars for public broadcasting were being used for the emergency transmissions necessary to keep fire, police, and other safety-related crews coordinated. The National Association of Home Builders pointed out that people had lost their homes and would probably need new ones at some point.

Circumstances change, often in ways that are completely out of your control. Upper management may decide that they won't be hiring for a certain job. A sales slump may mean that a potential customer won't need or want your service. Something dramatic may happen that grips the attention of the nation. Lobbyists for BP experienced this after the April 2010 oil spill that caused extensive environmental damage in the Gulf of Mexico. In an effort to manage the political fallout, they were forced to drop every other legislative project. For weeks, the oil spill was all anyone wanted to talk about, so BP and its business community partners talked about that.

No matter how fabulous your cause, sometimes things just happen that will either directly or indirectly impact your likelihood of success. You can mitigate the damage by recognizing these events as they occur and, where possible, finding ways to control those uncontrollable factors by connecting back to what matters to decision makers in the current environment.

Specific Takeaways

If you take away any lessons from this tactic they should be:

- Recognize when game-changing events occur.
- Don't waste time trying to shift attention away from those events and back to your issue, especially if your issue is unrelated.
- Control the uncontrollable by identifying the emerging message du jour and, where possible, capitalize on the opportunity by connecting your issue back to that message.

Tactic 45: What to Do if You Succeed

First, make sure you've really succeeded. Trust but verify was not only a credo of former president Ronald Reagan but also a rule to live by for Emily Sheketoff of the ALA. As discussed in the Introduction, when the Consumer Products Safety Commission (CPSC) agreed in principle to exempt children's books from their new lead regulations she was cautious. The ALA relaxed its campaign for the cause, but did not entirely stop. Not until CPSC released the specific language did she, as the saying goes, call off the dogs.

Lobbyists recognize that a yes isn't a true yes until the task is completed. For example, a legislator may agree to cosponsor a bill based on a lobbyist's request. But that agreement is simply the first step. If Congressman John Doe wants to cosponsor Jane Smith's bill, his first step is to tell his staff. Doe's staff person must find Smith's staff person and tell him or her to add Doe's name to the bill. Smith's staff person must provide a notice (signed by Representative Smith) to the parliamentarian's office indicating that Representative Doe would like to cosponsor the bill. Only then has the lobbyist truly succeeded.

In the influence game, words don't indicate success. Actions do. This is especially true in Washington, D.C., where words get thrown around—a lot. Those representing special interests always follow-up to ensure that the agreed-to action has really been taken. At the same time, they tend to relax the pressure a little. In most cases, the decision maker does not take the action they've agreed to for innocuous reasons, not because they are lying. They may simply need an occasional polite nudge, not the barrage that got them to agree with you in the first place.

As a small-business owner, I tend to think about this in the context of the simple act of sending an invoice to a client. The client has agreed to pay for our service (and in some cases the service has already been completed). We send an invoice. Unfortunately, some of our clients (I'm not naming names) do not complete the action of, well, paying, so we need to remind them. I never celebrate completing the sale until we've got the cash in hand.

Specific Takeaways

If you take away any lessons from this tactic they should be:

- Even after you get a yes, be sure the action is taken.
- Relax the pressure, without giving up completely.

- Never assign nefarious reasons for their lack of action. Sometimes it's just that they're busy.

- Be polite in your reminders. Don't harass them until they decide they don't want to deal with you and your cause any more.

Tactic 46: Don't Take Credit— Even if You Deserve It

Professional lobbyists are quick to praise and slow to give blame, especially where policymakers are involved. Despite the level of support materials or other resources they provided, lobbyists give all the credit for any success to the person or people who voted for (or against) their cause. As you might imagine, this approach makes it much easier to go back to that policymaker in the future.

For example, it's not uncommon for a legislator's office to make an announcement on their website or other public forum when a certain business or organization in their district has won a federal grant. In many cases, the legislator had nothing to do with the grant being awarded. It was the work of the person who wrote the proposal, the organization who lobbied for the grant, or the larger special interest who helped a local member get information about the program. Yet no one says to the legislator, "Hey, you had nothing to do with this." They say, "Hey, we're glad you're so supportive of this program. Could you please vote to continue its funding?"

When using this tactic in your own influence situation, think carefully about whether you can give credit to the decision maker for a positive outcome, even if it wasn't entirely their doing. Sure, you don't want to fawn over them or have someone else take all the credit for your good work. But, for example, occasionally making your boss look good with the client (even if you did most of the work to achieve a positive outcome) can help you move ahead.

Specific Takeaways

If you take away any lessons from this tactic they should be:

- Give others credit. Liberally.

- When others take credit for a good outcome, turn that into an opportunity to solicit their future support.

- Don't get too hung-up on making sure you get all the credit for your work, especially with those you're hoping will help you in the future.

Tactic 47: Say Thank You

My mother would be appalled at the lack of "thank you" note writing going on in the world (including by me, frankly). As a congressional staff person, I saved all the notes I received because they were so rare. At the end of several years, I had a very small stack, maybe about 25. Why so few? I don't think I was a horrible person to work with. I think it's because people didn't take the time. But I remembered those who did and, believe me, they received preferential treatment. In fact, my favorite thank-yous were those that were sent to my boss with a note indicating how helpful I had been. They made me look good.

At the same time, lobbyists aren't obsequious. Legislators recognize insincerity and they enjoy it about as much as anyone else might. Special interests offer their thanks only when in earnest, and at a level appropriate to the situation. For example, when members of Congress made public statements in the Congressional Record regarding World Stroke Day (an educational effort supported by a variety of stroke-associated groups nationwide), the National Stroke Association quickly took steps through social media channels to let all of its 50,000 members know.

The National Stroke Association provided this information to its advocates because of these legislators' strong leadership on their issues, even though it had been National Stroke Association staff who helped write the statements. Note that they did not (and frankly could not) show their support through campaign contributions, which is, of course, the way we think most legislators like to be thanked.

Those who help you are spending their time, money, and resources to do so—even if you don't get what you want. The time you take to write a simple note probably pales in comparison. From a purely selfish perspective, also remember that thank-yous help you get in good with your audience. People remember them because they are so rare.

Congressman Earl Blumenauer (D-OR) writes thank-you notes on the airplane as he goes back and forth between D.C. and his district several times a month. He would often come back with stacks of cards for us to mail. They ranged from brief expressions of gratitude for a visit to longer and more personal letters. Most important, he felt sincerely grateful that people cared enough about his work to spend time with him. His thank-yous are from the heart.

And they are the right thing to do. My mom would approve.

Specific Takeaways

If you take away any lessons from this tactic they should be:

- Figure out who you should thank. Usually that's anyone who took time, money, resources, or even put their reputation at stake to help you.

- Be sincere in your thank-yous. Don't try to curry favor by thanking people who really shouldn't be thanked.

- Find a way to thank them through a note or a phone call, if possible in a way that makes them look good with their superiors.

- Be grateful for any help, even if you don't get what you want.

Tactic 48: Avoid Failure by Redefining Success

Failure happens, at least in the short term. As Winston Churchill so aptly pointed out, "Success consists of going from failure to failure without loss of enthusiasm." Many people, even powerful lobbyists, fail repeatedly. When this happens, they pick themselves up, dust themselves off, and recognize that if they persevere, some kind of success will come. It may not be the vision of success they started out with, but it will be success nonetheless.

The unscrupulous ones even welcome failure, as it means more paying work for them in the long run. I hate to say it, but it's true.

You can reduce the potential for failure by engaging in the tactics outlined in this book. If you establish realistic goals (see Tactic 3), know your competition, know your audience, develop an effective campaign plan, and deliver your message powerfully, strategically, and with sincerity, your chances of success increase exponentially. That said, external forces—the political environment, the economy, or even public perception—can have negative impacts.

The American Library Association experienced this when lobbying on a proposal to identify school librarians as a specific job category to be favored by legislation (the American Jobs Act) to promote job creation. President Barack Obama indicated that he strongly supported expanding professional positions associated with education and, frankly, those not entirely focused on the male-dominated fields of construction and housing. Armed with a message about the desire to keep school librarians working, and a force of 74,000 school and other librarians and supporters nationwide to deliver the message, the issue seemed to be a slam dunk.

They got nowhere. No one would even listen to their proposals. And yet many construction-oriented shovel-ready projects were included in the legislation. The reasons why they were unable to get any traction on the issue completely eluded them.

But what did they do? They sought another avenue for their goal, asking legislators to include language referring to the importance of school librarians in an education reform bill. Although the bill has not yet been considered (as of spring 2012), the ALA has found another potential means of succeeding and continues to carry on.

As part of the effort the ALA has also set a series of goals, many of which they have more control over. Rather than relying on the ever-changing legislative environment to determine success or failure, they established interim goals related to the steps *they* could take to eventually achieve success. For example, they set targets for the number of librarians responding to action alerts or conducting library visits. In this way, they focused on internal goals, not external. For your situation, that may mean the number of sales calls or interviews, or even a target date by which you'll save a specific amount of money toward your goal. In other words, it's up to you to control your own fate.

While moving toward your long-term success, just remind yourself that as setbacks happen, you have not yet failed: you just have not yet succeeded. I realize that sounds like political double-talk, and maybe it is. But in D.C., as in the real world, those playing the influence game must have this perspective or, frankly, they would constantly be disappointed. Believe me, there are a lot of people in Washington, D.C., who, despite years of effort, have not yet succeeded on their policy issue.

Specific Takeaways

If you take away any lessons from this tactic they should be:

- Failure is not permanent: it's a short-term status.
- Redefine success in ways that depend on *your* action, not the external environment.
- You control your fate, not those you're trying to influence.

Tactic 49: Really Don't Do These Five Things

Maybe it's cheating to have the 49th tactic be really five separate things, but they are so important I couldn't resist. Regardless of which tactics you use to further your influence effort, you won't get far if you do any of the following five things.

Number 5: Don't Insult the Decision Maker or Anyone Surrounding the Decision Maker

In Washington, D.C., this translates into comments like:

> "I thought I was going to get to meet with the congressman. Why do I have to meet with *just you?*" (See Tactic 20 for more on this totally offensive comment.)
>
> "I know you receive campaign contributions for your votes, so you'll never agree with me, but I thought I'd come talk to you anyway."
>
> "You must be lying to me. I heard Jon Stewart of *The Daily Show* say otherwise." (I love Jon Stewart and his cadre of correspondents, by the way. They just aren't always the most accurate source of information. There's a reason it's described as a "fake" news show, albeit a hysterical one.)

Bradford Fitch of the Congressional Management Foundation tells the story of a group that was very irritated with a particular member of Congress about his position on a controversial small-business issue. The group decided to attend a town hall meeting to express their disappointment and, when the legislator arrived, engaged in a choreographed display of holding an actual noose around their neck and pointing at the legislator. They believed it showed their commitment to the issue. The legislator believed they'd gone over the top.

In short, remember that there are things you might think inside your head, but don't say them. Preserve positive relationships so you can live to fight another day if necessary.

Number 4: Don't Interrupt the Decision Maker with Communications That Are Not Really High Priority

Statements related to this no-no include the following: "Since it's always better to talk in person I thought I'd come over," or "I don't care if she's on a conference call, I must speak to her now," or "I sent you this e-mail an hour ago, why haven't you responded?" I worked with someone once who marked every e-mail she sent as high priority. This made it very difficult to know which missives really were important.

It's okay to stop by, drop off some materials with a relevant staff person, and let them know of your interest in the issue. It's not okay to camp out in their doorway and demand that someone talk to you.

Number 3: Don't Be Vague about Your Goals

It's very difficult to find your target audience, know the arena, find surrogates, develop a message, and deliver that message to the right people if you don't know what you want. Having a SMART goal forms the foundation of everything else. You may not need to articulate that goal to everyone all the time, but you still need to know what it is. Without a goal, you'll never know if you're getting to yes!

Number 2: Don't Not Know What You're Talking About

Nothing discourages someone from listening to you more than communication that is peppered with inaccuracies. Take steps to learn everything you need to know about your cause, including the benefits and downsides of your proposed solution to a problem. If you don't know the answer to a question, say, "I don't know; I'll get back to you." Then do it.

Number 1: Don't Give Up

As Dave Wenhold's experience with the court reporters shows (see the section on "Perseverence" in Chapter 1), it can take years to move a relatively minor program through the legislative process, even with a variety of powerful tools at your disposal. In the real world, many decisions may take a similarly long time. I've certainly experienced communicating with a potential client over the course of years before they hired me. But had I given up just one day before I got the call, I would not have gotten the business. Persistence works.

Tactic 50: Have Fun

To end on a positive note, remember that no influence-effort situation should feel like a trip to the dentist (sorry dentists!). The goal of your campaign should be to achieve a goal you really, really, *really* want to achieve. If it starts feeling like a chore, you're probably on the wrong track. From getting that dream job to landing that big client to effecting that important policy change, getting to yes isn't always easy. But when you finally get there, it should be hugely satisfying. And if you use just some of the tactics outlined in this book, you'll get there. I promise.

Index